MEMORABLE MOMENTS
IN MOTOR RACING

MEMORABLE MOMENTS
IN MOTOR RACING

LEGENDS AND PERSONALITIES
TELL THEIR STORIES

PREFACE BY DAVID COULTHARD
COMPILED BY MIKE JIGGLE
EDITED BY DAVID BARZILAY

CYANBOOKS   Barzilay

First published in Great Britain in 2005 by
Cyan Books, an imprint of

Cyan Communications Limited
119 Wardour Street
London W1F 0UW
T: +44 (0)20 7565 6120
F: +44 (0)20 7565 6121
E: sales@cyanbooks.com
www.cyanbooks.com

and

Barzilay Associates
12 York Gate
London NW1 4QS
T: +44 (0)20 7544 8980
E: david@barzilay.co.uk

A CIP record for this book is available from the British Library

ISBN 1-904879-58-6

Book design by So... *www.soitbegins.co.uk*

Printed by in Great Britain by
Cambrian Printers, Aberystwyth

Bound in Great Britain by
TJ International, Padstow, Cornwall

Contents

Foreword by David Coulthard

Memorable Moments in Motor Racing contains the personal thoughts and opinions of some of the greatest drivers of recent years and provides a unique insight into what they regard their finest moments.

Like me, some of the drivers who have participated have not chosen what spectators, commentators, or fans of the sport would see as an obvious career highlight into their memorable moments.

That's the point of the book, it's an insight into the private thoughts of these drivers and it gives the reader the chance to share something very personal with them.

As its not interview lead, what follows is a collection of spontaneous remarks made by some of the sports great characters and in purchasing and reading this book you have joined them in contributing to a worthy cause.

Please read on and enjoy.

Best wishes,

David Coulthard

All book royalties will be donated to:

Providing advice, information, medical equipment and 24-hour support for those who suffer respiratory problems. *www.thebreathingcharity.org.uk*

Preface and Acknowledgements by Mike Jiggle

As a long time follower of motor racing, I have always wanted to know what made some of my on-track heroes tick. Is it something to do with the psyche of the professional athlete? Competitiveness and the desire to win seem to be the ultimate attributes required. Many have these qualities by the bucket-load. As one grows older it becomes clear that these superhuman men and women are just like the rest of us, mere mortals, who, as with other professionals, have a particular gift which elevates them above others in their field, a certain excellence. However, do they think as we do? We look back and remember a tremendous race, or a great over-taking manoeuvre. What makes those, less successful or on the periphery of the sport, keep going? What is motor racing from their perspective? It surely isn't just the love of the sport — or is it?

I am fortunate to have access to the "inside" so I thought of asking, "What is one of your most memorable moments in motor racing." My question, which may go some way to satisfying my curiosity, was asked to many. Those considered legends, those who are at the forefront today, those who participate at lower levels, those who the sport depend on to allow the racing and those who talk about it. From the responses you will find some predictable, some unpredictable, some to be smiled upon and some of a more serious nature. All make very interesting reading.

I had initially thought to put these "moments" together as an autograph book with
a difference, which would be ultimately auctioned. As this was rather restricting in its
circulation, the moments are published for all to read. For this, I would like to give special
thanks to the following people who have made a considerable contribution to the making
of this book:

- To all those who returned their pages suitably inscribed with their "moment."
- To David Coulthard for being the first contributor and writing the foreword.
- To Michael Turner and Jim Bamber for supplying new and original artwork.
- To James Beckett and the British Racing Drivers Club.
- To Eileen Circuit at the NARA office for dealing with all the extra post and phone calls.
- To Ed McDonough for lending an ear of advice (day or night).
- To Cyan Books and David Barzilay without whom the book would not have been published.
    Throughout this project I have had the love and support of my wife, Ann, and my
children, Kelvin, Krys, Kary, and Keith, without whom none of this would have been possible.

The royalties of this book, together with the auction value of the original manuscripts will
be donated to NARA – The Breathing Charity.

Introduction by David Barzilay

For Mike Jiggle, compiling this book has been a real labour of love. As a motor racing enthusiast of many years standing he has attended hundreds of race meetings around the world and has got to meet and know many of its personalities.

In 1984, following personal experiences, Mike and his wife Ann, together with others, started NARA – The Breathing Charity, which provides medical equipment and support to those suffering breathing difficulties. Individuals who benefit from this work range from the very young to the elderly. The assistance given is in collaboration with medical agencies and benefits both the patient and their family. As with most charities, raising money is always an issue and in recent years, Mike has combined his love of motor racing and his role as coordinator for the charity to raise money.

For the past six years as Mike has travelled to circuits and met drivers, he has asked them to write down for him their favourite motor racing moment. The initial intention was simply to provide a unique book of autographed moments that could be auctioned for the charity. But as time went on, and more and more drivers shared with Mike moments that had influenced their careers, he decided that perhaps the entries would make a book.

While this was under way, Mike decided to organise a series of motor racing charity dinners to raise money for NARA. The first was to recognise Vanwall and then, in 2004, a charity dinner to recognise the achievements of John Surtees, the only man to win world championships on both two wheels and four. It was at this dinner that I met Mike and saw that he was a man with a mission.

When Mike first set off on his quest he would simply ask for an autograph but quickly realised that this told nothing about that particular person. "An autograph simply states that a particular person has put his or her mark on a piece of paper, book or item of memorabilia," said Mike. Standing in line or hunting round the pits at places like Goodwood, Mike became annoyed as he saw motor racing personalities being asked for an autograph, only to then hear the recipient ask "Who was that?" As Mike puts it, "What is the point of asking for something if you are not sure what it is you have?" So, a book was born and Mike started to ask motor racing personalities what their memorable moment was. What started out as an idea for an autograph book had suddenly turned into a unique book of moments stretching back well over 60 years.

Many of the names that appear are household names; others are not. But they are all people who made a huge impact on the sport. From the man who painted the numbers on the cars at the start of a Grand Prix to Sir Stirling Moss stating that his most memorable moment was winning the Mille Miglia in 1955.

What Mike wanted was an eclectic list of contributors, not just every day household names, but those whose contribution to the sport go unnoticed, like the late Ernie Knott. A local signwriter by trade, Ernie was asked to paint the numbers on the cars at Silverstone race meetings in the very early years of the circuit. In later years he was in charge of the tow truck. It was Ernie that pulled Jackie Stewart's Tyrrell from the straw bails at Copse Corner in the 1973 British Grand Prix. Mike met Ernie a few months prior to his death, a charming man with many stories to tell about the early days of motor racing.

Mike concluded that many stories went untold because it was felt that people like Ernie had no value. Mike felt it was important that the people behind the scenes, who had made it possible for the champions to race, had their opportunity to tell their stories.

Mike of course includes moments from the greats in motor racing like Moss, Mansell and Schumacher but makes the point that the moments themselves are not supposed to be the indelible mark of the personality concerned, merely one of the many moments in time they recall with affection or otherwise.

Some have gone on to greater things since giving their memorable moment. Michael Schumacher, for instance, recalls his first championship for Ferrari but has gone on to win four more, becoming the only person to win seven world championships.

The stories relate to the time that they were given and other incidents may have happened since. However, David Coulthard tells his story about an F3 race in Macau – and was quite adamant that whatever he achieved in Formula One or motor racing, this was a defining moment for him and could not be bettered.

Mike wanted a lasting tribute to those who are no longer with us and in the six years that it has taken Mike to compile this book, some of the contributors have died. People like the late Mort Morris-Goodall who was the founder of the Aston Martin Owners Club and indeed raced Aston Martins at Le Mans on eight occasions. He had sent two letters to Mike asking him to choose which story he wanted. Asking about what would happen to the story and hoping for a copy of the book when it was published, he remarked, "Hope you get it done by Christmas, old boy, I'm feeling a bit tired these days and may fall off the perch before too long." Mike was a bit taken aback but recalled that Mort said it with a smile on his face and happiness in his heart. Mort did die a few months later – not a man whose name immediately springs to mind, but a stalwart of the sport in its infancy.

It seemed right for me to ask Mike what his memorable moment has been. Apart from a few kart races, and taking a few lessons with the Jim Russell Racing Drivers School in the early 1970s, he feels very privileged to have presented Sir Stirling Moss and Tony Brooks with the Fred G. Craner Memorial Trophy. This trophy is awarded to the British or Commonwealth driver of a British car placed highest in the finishing order of the British Grand Prix. The trophy was to be presented to them at Aintree in 1957 after their victorious Vanwall drive. For some reason, it was never presented and only Stirling's name had been put on the trophy. However, the presentation was finally made at the charity Vanwall Victory dinner at the Guildhall, Northampton in 2002 with Tony's name added. Mike was delighted.

Perhaps Mike Jiggle's most memorable moment has been to compile this book in the first place. It is a unique record of the famous and not so famous. Those that have made motor racing what it is today. In an effort to keep the whole thing going Mike insisted that we the publishers, Cyan Books and Barzilay Associates, include some blank pages at the back so that you the readers can collect your own motor racing autographs and moments in the years to come.

The original manuscripts for this book, which form a unique autograph book in themselves, have been bound and will be auctioned with all the proceeds going to NARA – The Breathing Charity.

MEMORABLE
MOMENTS IN
MOTOR RACING
STARTS HERE

1 **Laurent Aiello** *Touring Car Champion*
Winning the BTCC (British Touring Car Championship) in 1999.

2 **Pentti Airikkala** *Rally driver*
Winning the RAC Rally in 1989 against all the odds.

3 **Jean Alesi** *Formula One driver*
Without any doubt, in Canada in 1993, where I won my only Grand Prix.

Phillipe Alliot *Formula One driver*

Firstly, my two seasons in 1991 and 1992 with Jean Todt and the Peugeot 905. Also when I drove the McLaren both in testing and, of course, in my only race for them in Hungary in 1994. But above all this, it must be my first victory in Formula Renault.

⑤ Cliff Allison *Formula One driver*

In practice for the German Grand Prix in 1959, I was driving a Ferrari 246 with
Tony Brooks, Dan Gurney and Phil Hill. I was a little off-the-pace and, in a special
effort, I drifted the car around on the brick-banking with the nose of the car pointing
to the centre and full opposite lock. It was a very hairy experience but rewarding,
with a lap of 147mph.

Fernando Alonso *Formula One driver*

I think it was my pole position in Malaysia. However, I look forward to one day winning my home Grand Prix. Any win I have though is memorable, and winning for Renault is wonderful!

Mario Andretti Formula *One World Champion/Indy 500 winner*

The 1986 Pocono 500 race weekend. My son Jeff started and won his Indy Lights race from the pole on Saturday. The next day in the Champ Car race with [my other son] Michael on pole, I won the Pocono 500 making a clean sweep for the Andretti family.

8 **Bob Ansell** *Grand Prix driver*

It was in the British Empire Trophy 1948 on the Isle of Man driving my 4CL Maserati. Three miles ahead of the field, my brakes failed going downhill into Oncan. The race was eventually won by my late cousin Geoffrey in my old ERA R4B so the trophy was kept in the family.

9 **Michael Anthony** *Sportscar driver*

When I went into the hairpin at Rouen and found I had no brakes!!!

René Arnoux *Formula One driver*

Just motor racing! However, I think in Dijon in 1979 at the French Grand Prix, where I raced with Villeneuve and we were fighting for second place. In the last six laps we must have touched wheels six times each lap. Everyone remembers this race. Unfortunately for poor Jabouille, everyone remembers who came second and third but not who won the race.

Cyril Atkins *Mechanic*

In 1950, I joined Tony Vandervell's team. Tony became fed up with red cars
winning all the races so he decided to build his own car, the Vanwall. After years
of domination by Ferrari, we won the World Championship in 1959. Then I moved
on to BRM and won the Championship *again* with Graham Hill.

Rowan Atkinson *Actor/Historic racing driver*

Remembering listening to the Monaco Grand Prix when Senna and Mansell were duelling for first place. Both of them at that time were at the top of their powers. Of course Mansell could not get past Senna but the most intriguing part for me was listening rather than watching and imagining their fight. The commentary was more riveting and exciting than it could ever be by just watching it. It taught me that the most visual events well described can be more exciting than watching the reality.

Richard Attwood *Formula One driver*

My invitation to drive for BRM in the 1968 Monaco Grand Prix came quite late after Mike Spence was killed during qualifying for the Indianapolis 500. (Initially, BRM may have thought of only entering one car.) I arrived at Nice airport in time for the first qualifying session and met Jean and Louis Stanley, part of the Owen Racing Organisation. They asked me why I was there. I replied that I would be driving the second BRM and Pedro Rodriguez would be my team-mate. (Communications were not like they are today. There was no TV and there was a general strike across France at that time, so that's why they didn't know about my impending drive.)

For whatever reason, my official works BRM entry was changed and ultimately entered under the "private" team of "Reg Parnell Racing" which was run by his son Tim. The private entry duly finished second (equalling BRM's best result that year) with the lap record for good measure. Had the results been known beforehand, the original entry might not have been changed!

14 **Julian Bailey** *Formula One driver*
Signing my contract with Ken Tyrrell and driving away
from the factory knowing I was now a Formula One driver.

15 **Sir Gawaine Baillie** *Saloon Car driver*
Being in front of Stirling Moss in my Jaguar saloon car even though, as happened,
he passed me soon afterwards.

16 **Mauro Baldi** *Formula One driver*
Racing in the 1998 season for the Doran/Moretti team and driving the Ferrari
333SP with Didier Theys and Giampiero Moretti. I won the Daytona 24 Hours,
the Sebring 12 Hours and the Watkins Glen 6 Hours, seizing the so-called "Triple
Crown." We were the first team ever in the history of American motor racing to
achieve this result. I will always remember those fantastic moments.

Jim Bamber *Cartoonist*

My first ride in a works rally car in May 1996. It was going to be with Gwyndaf Evans. At the time I thanked my lucky stars it wasn't going to be with Malcolm Wilson. If it had been Wilson he would have done his utmost to make me sick to take revenge for all the times I had made fun of him in my cartoons. But in this works Ford Escort on a mountainside somewhere north of Sanremo it was going to be Gwyndaf who would give me just a small taste of what real rally car could do.

Two point three kilometres of narrow twisting tarmac. On one side rock – just rock. The other side – a long way down – was another part of Italy. A part I had no interest in exploring. Gwyndaf was saying something but I was miles away looking at the road. There were no straight bits to talk about, it was all bends. Some were blind, that's why we were coasting to check if the road was safe for the run back up the hill. At the bottom of the hill was a small village. There was no space to turn, nothing, the road was too narrow, with a sheer drop on my right and suddenly we were facing the other way! No drama, no noise, no real sense that we had just spun through 180 degrees and we were off. The blue touch paper had been lit and if I still had been a Catholic I would have crossed myself!

I can't tell you how fast we were going. I can't even tell you what gear Gwyndaf was in. It took all my concentration and willpower to simply keep my head from falling off my shoulders. When the throttle pedal was clamped to the metal I found myself staring at the roof and when the brake was crunched, which seemed to be every bloody second, my eyeballs were left staring at my shoes. Of my short time in the car it was the brakes that impressed me most. I had expected the run to be fast. I had expected it to be exciting and scary. What I did not expect, and my neck was still stiff four days later because of it, was the incredible power of the brakes.

Maybe I was impressed by the brakes but Gwyndaf wasn't. The balance during the run was wrong. We had been lifting a back wheel. More testing would be needed to sort it out but it thankfully not with me on board. Cue chicken noises. As we came to a stop, the Ford mechanics gathered round the car laughing and pointing. I couldn't think why until Gwyndaf pointed out that for most of the run I had unwittingly been sounding the horn which is, of course, fitted to the co-drivers footrest! Aaaaaaargh!

18 **Warwick Banks** *Saloon Car/Sportscar driver*

It was in 1964, having to do a four-hour race in a works Mini Cooper round a bumpy Monza banking when our team manager, Ken Tyrrell, would not let me out of the car for anything!!! However, we won the class and the European Saloon Car Championship.

19 **Olivier Beretta** *Formula One driver*

The Grand Prix of Monaco in 1994. I was born in this little country and I grew up in my parents' apartment which is on the circuit. For years I watched the Formula One Grand Prix. I had the great opportunity to race and finish in eighth position for the Larrousse Formula One team.

20 **Tom Barnard** *Mechanic*

When I was having dinner with Archie Scott-Brown and Jack Fairman at the famous Steering Wheel Club in London in November 1957.

We had been talking about the season that had just ended and Archie suddenly said that he and Jack would like to propose me for the British Racing Drivers' Club. In the 1950s this was an enormous honour and with two such famous sponsors my nomination was duly accepted. Six months later, Archie died after a terrible accident at the Spa racing circuit in Belgium and within a fortnight I had hung up my helmet and retired. Archie had overcome appalling physical deformities to become one of the finest drivers of his generation. His courage in the face of these disabilities remains an example and an encouragement to anyone suffering from handicaps however large, however small.

21 **Rubens Barrichello** *Formula One driver*

The 1999 Brazilian Grand Prix was the most satisfying and memorable moment of my Formula One career to date because I was able to perform really well under a lot of pressure. I felt that having led my own Grand Prix after qualifying third on the grid, my own people had began to believe in me. Finishing second in Monaco in 1997 was also an emotional moment for both myself and the Stewart team, because it was our first podium finish, but the experience in Brazil for me personally was very special.

22 **Raymond Baxter** *Commentator/Spitfire pilot*

The 1961 Monaco Grand Prix. Doing the BBC commentary I watched Stirling Moss alone hold off and beat the three pursuing Ferraris, driving Rob Walker's privately entered Lotus. Those were the days!!!

23 **Mike Beckwith** *Sportscar driver*
Winning the 1966 Vigorelli Trophy at Monza by half a car's length from Jonathan
Williams. I was also lucky to have raced with the great Jim Clark finishing second
behind him in the sportscar race in 1963 driving the Lotus 23B.

24 **Derek Bell** *Formula One driver/Le Mans winner*
Leading at the Le Mans 24 Hour race in 1995 in my McLaren (Harrods).
We ultimately finished third. Driving with my son Justin (plus Andy Wallace)
and to be in on the winner's rostrum.

(25) Ralph Bellamy *Designer*

Jacky Ickx's pit stop to change from wet to dry tyres on the 24th lap of the Spanish Grand Prix at Jarama in 1974. The car was waved away with the wheel wrench still attached to the wheel nut. As the car drove forward the wheel nut came undone and the wheel fell off with the car coming to halt in Tim Schenken's pit halfway down the pit road. The wheel was quickly replaced but, in the panic to start the car, the fire extinguisher button in the cockpit was pressed instead of the starter button. A cloud of white gas erupted from the cockpit and was drawn into the engine air inlet during subsequent unsuccessful attempts to restart the engine. Due to a chemical reaction beyond my understanding it seems that the simple process of passing the extinguishant gas through a hot internal combustion engine causes its volume and density to increase a thousandfold. In a very short time, Tim Schenken's pit and the pit road then even the race track were obscured by an enormous cloud of white smoke. The result was chaos. Not a lap chart in the pit road survived this incident. I think that anybody who was there that day will remember this incident as one of the most chaotic and comical pit-stops of all time.

26 **Ray Bellm** *Sportscar driver*
Winning the 1996 World GT Championship in a McLaren F1 GTR.

27 **Jean-Pierre Beltoise** *Formula One driver*
My victory at Monaco with the V12 Marlboro BRM in 1972.

28 **Gerhard Berger** *Formula One driver*

When I got into Formula One and learned to use the turbo engine to the maximum. The way you drive a normal car around a corner is completely different to the way you control a turbo. I remember back in 1986 and 1987 when the top turbo engines were pushing out 1400 horsepower and the cars had big, sticky qualifying tyres. Qualifying in those days was the most exciting thing. Far, far more than it is now. But today a quick qualifying lap time, compared to a medium qualifying lap time, is the result of putting a row of details together; to work everything on a fine line, snatching a few metres under braking, putting the car through the corner on the limit, trying not to get it too far sideways, not to slow the car down too much and to get just the right moment to open the throttle, and in the end, if you get the small details right, then you are one-tenth quicker, maybe even two-tenths quicker. Today, one second can cover eight to ten cars.

In the turbo days these fine details didn't matter because the cars was so brutal with all that horsepower boosted by the turbo. Okay, with the delays of the turbo you had to brake late, but when you finished braking you had to be already full on the throttle as you entered the corner because the delay in turbo response meant it wouldn't kick in until the corner was finished. If, for any reason, the turbo power came in just two metres too early, the result was a big power slide coming out. But you could still control the big power slide with the throttle and you had so much power you could still catch up again. The slide wouldn't ruin your next straight. Whereas these days, with current cars, when you have a big slide out of the corner the next straight is dead because you don't have the power to bring back the speed. So it was not a question of details, it was a question of timing and bigger balls!!! Today, the guys wouldn't believe what it was like to go around Monte Carlo with those engines!

Mike "Herbie" Blash *Team Manager*

The day that Nelson Piquet won the World Championship in 1983 with our very small Brabham BMW team. We went into the last race in South Africa behind Renault who were already convinced they had the Championship won. It really was a David and Goliath situation and we proved that the Davids of this world can win!

Jean Bloxham *Sportscar driver*

In 1955, being made a member of the prestigious British Racing Drivers' Club!

Jimmy Blumer *Sportscar/Racing driver*

At Spa, I went off backwards into the biggest rock at Eau Rouge. Another car collected me. Then I remember being collected by an ambulance, and its woman driver passed most of the other competitors around the circuit. I remember asking for cognac and only being given Spa water! Not nice. I have had many, many memorable moments. I remember winning the Whitsun Trophy at Goodwood some 40 years ago.

32 **Bill Blythe** *Mechanic*

Watching the Italian Grand Prix at Monza in 1953. There were six Ferraris and six Maseratis entered and Ascari made pole position by half a second from Fangio. From the start Ascari went into the lead, and then throughout the race the four cars raced wheel to wheel, Ascari and Farina (Ferrari) and Fangio and Marimon (Maserati), with no more than three seconds covering the entire bunch. Stirling Moss was holding fifth place in a very special Cooper Alta running on nitromethane before retirement with various troubles.

Ascari was leading by a length from Farina as they went into the last lap, Marimon behind them, then Fangio. Coming into the last bend, Ascari spun off. Marimon hit him, putting both of them out. Farina swerved to avoid them, giving Fangio a small gap into which he shot, roaring down the finishing straight to an unexpected but very popular win.

33 **Bob Bondurant** *Formula One driver*

Racing at Le Mans in 1964 with Dan Gurney in a Cobra. The car was good, Dan was good, and I was good and we won the GT category finishing fourth overall behind three Ferrari prototypes. A very, very, very wonderful moment.

34 **David Brabham** *Formula One driver*

The 1987 Australian Formula Two Gold Star race at the Adelaide Grand Prix.
I started 35th on the grid after a really bad qualifying session, I'd also had an
argument with my Dad before the race. I was really upset and I was still mad when
I got into the car for the race. I won the race!

Sir Jack Brabham *Three times Formula One World Champion*
Winning the French Grand Prix at Reims in 1966 which was our first win in the
Australian-made Repco Brabham car and engine which was the forerunner to
winning my third World Championship.

36 **Annie Bradshaw** *Public relations officer*
Being in Japan when Damon Hill won his World Championship.

37 **Ross Brawn** *Technical Director*
One of my most memorable moments in motor racing I hope is still to come.
A World Drivers' Championship with Ferrari.

38 **Nick Brittan** *Saloon Car driver*
My first race on the South circuit of the Nürburgring 1967. The degree of difficulty associated with this circuit was legendary. In the early laps of practice I noticed a neat row of Christmas trees about four feet tall on the outside of a tricky downhill left-hander. What a cute place to grow Christmas trees I thought. On the last lap of practice, eager to set a good time, I drifted wide on that corner and was shattered to discover that the cute little Christmas trees were the tops of 40ft tall pine trees growing in the valley below. Gulp!!!!

39 **Tony Brooks** *Formula One driver*

Receiving the letter from Aston Martin in 1955 inviting me to join their works team that year. I was a club driver at the time and joining the Aston team was the springboard for my motor racing career. A team member asked me to drive his private Formula Two Connaught in half a dozen national events which led to the invitation to drive the works Connaught at Syracuse in October 1955 – my first Formula One drive. This was the first Grand Prix victory by a British car and driver for 32 years and it launched my Formula One career.

40 **Alan Brown** *Formula One driver*

It was, I suppose, winning the British Empire Trophy in 1954 in a Cooper Bristol. You know, motor racing is the best sport in the world. I also remember being at Silverstone in 1956 and thinking it's time to give up so I just stopped for no particular reason other than I ran out of steam.

Peter Browning *Race Director*

At the start of the Rothmans 50000 held at Brands Hatch in 1972. I had only recently joined the British Racing and Sports Car Club as their executive director and this was to be one of my first jobs as a somewhat young and inexperienced clerk of the course.

The Rothmans 50000 was a unique event offering a prize fund of £50,000 and was open to all-comers: Formula One, Indy cars, Formula 5000 and indeed any other competitive single-seater or sportscar. The idea was to stage a confrontation between Formula One and Indy cars but the entry was somewhat disappointing and failed to attract any truly top teams other than one serious Grand Prix entry for Emerson Fittipaldi driving the dominating and successful JPS Lotus.

The event was unusual in that there was no start money and the total prize fund was offered for grid positions, lap leaders and final overall placings. Typically, Team Lotus did not agree with this and after a lot of behind-the-scenes haggling, I was forced to agree to some form of minimum guarantee should Emerson fail to do well. There was also the inevitable tiresome haggle with Lotus over free admission tickets and pit passes, etc. This was all carried out with a certain amount of good humoured gamesmanship and I was well aware that Team Lotus were taking full advantage of negotiating with a novice clerk of the course. Needless to say Emerson dominated practice and took the considerable bonus for pole position.

The event was to have a rolling start and I had proudly placed my Ford Granada in front of the grid with some trepidation of having to perform in front of such illustrious company. After the three-minute signal I nonchalantly walked to the car, got in it, closed the door only to discover that the ignition key was missing. Panic! I knew I had left the key in the ignition but nevertheless quickly searched my pockets without success. It was only when I got out of the car that I spotted a Team Lotus mechanic standing on the other side of the Armco on the start-line dangling my car keys! I retrieved them without showing too much emotion and when I glanced back at Emerson, I could see from his laughter that he was in on the joke. After the race, which of course Emerson won with Lotus taking a major share of the £50,000 prize fund, he did at least offer to buy me a beer to apologise for the rotten trick.

Martin Brundle *Formula One driver/Le Mans winner*
Winning in Le Mans with Jaguar in 1990. Standing on the podium with a tired, emotional but ecstatic team and seeing the sea of happy fans waving their Union Jack flags below. Enjoying the good days to the full, which helps you through the inevitable bad days.

Norman Burkinshaw *Mechanic*
Being the chief mechanic on Tony Brooks' Vanwall. I had the honour of being given the mechanics award in 1958 by the L'AMAC (Paris) after Mr Vandervell had won the Constructors Championship for that year. The first win was at Aintree in 1957 which started the ball rolling for us.

44 Richard Burns *World Rally Champion*
Finishing the Hong Kong to Beijing Rally in 1996, the last ever running of the rally, to a crowd of literally hundreds of thousands of people in Tiananmen Square and on the steps of the Great Hall of the People.

45 Kelvin Burt *Sportscar driver*
When I raced GT cars in Japan in 1998. Every practice and race day we had to report early in the morning for a pointless medical, which included blood pressure, urine test, balancing on one leg, grip strength test, etc, etc. None of this was relevant to our driving as records and comparisons were not kept and it was annoying to have to arrive earlier just for this. So one time as a joke I replaced my urine sample with orange squash. The nurse looked surprised that the beaker was full to the top, so I drank some. She still tested it and said it was OK!!!!

46 **Patsy Burt** *National Sprint Champion*

Some of my most memorable moments in motor-racing were:

1955. Waiting to start a rally with the Aston DB 2/4, and a nearby voice saying, "Look! A woman driving. What a waste of a beautiful car!" I have since tried hard not to waste it!

1957. 1,000 km at the Nürburgring (MG). Retired early!

1959. RAC Hill Climb Championship (Cooper 1.5). Fourth overall.

1962. Being elected to the BRDC. Joining father and uncle (Eric and Stewart) as the third member of the family to qualify.

1968. Brighton Speed trials. Outright one kilometre course record which then stood for seven years (4.4 McLaren Oldsmobile).

1970. RAC National Sprint Champion. The first woman to win a national title (4.4 McLaren Automobile).

Above all, the excitement of competing and the enjoyment of the many friends I have made across the world.

Alistair Caldwell *Technical Director*

Winning and then losing the British Grand Prix in 1976. On the first lap of the race
at Brands Hatch the two Ferrari team cars of Lauda and Regazzoni collided taking
off half the field including James Hunt in his McLaren. Though his car was damaged,
James carried on in the race until it was stopped. We initially put his spare car on
the grid knowing this was not permitted under the rules. We joined in with Ferrari
and others who also had spare cars on the grid, arguing that they should be allowed
to start. Meanwhile, we were already repairing the original race car, when this was
finished we put it back on the grid and to Ferrari's chagrin won the race. Sadly,
months later, the FIA took away these hard won points in their all too usual cynical
decisions, but happily we still won the World Championship.

Ivan Capelli *Formula One driver*

France 1990, when we did the Grand Prix of France, that for me was the best part
of my racing career in Formula One. We led the Grand Prix for 46 laps and could
have gone on to win. We had a problem on the last two laps with oil pressure which
made me slow down a lot. The engine was nearly broken. The Leyton House team
was a small team but we had many good people like Gustav Brunner and Mario
Illien. Adrian Newey was the designer of the car. He left the team and has gone on
to be one of the greatest Formula One car designers ever.

THERE IS ALWAYS A START AND A FINISH
HAPPINESS AND SADNESS
BIRTH AND DEATH
LOVE AND HATE
   WITHOUT A START, THERE IS NEVER A FINISH
   WITHOUT SADNESS, THERE IS NEVER HAPPINESS
   WITHOUT BIRTH, THERE IS NEVER DEATH
   AND WITHOUT KNOWING HATE
   NO ONE CAN UNDERSTAND LOVE
NATURE HAS ITS CYCLE AND THERE IS
NO STRENGTH GREATER THAN NATURE
YOU MUST NEVER LOOSE THE STRENGTH
WITHIN YOUR SELF.

I WILL NEVER FORGET YOU

1987 - 88 - 89 - 90 - 91

49 **Dindo Capello** *Le Mans winner*

I have some good memories. One of the best was the victory of Allan McNish and me
in Mosport. This was probably the closest ever finish in the motor sport sportscar
story, just one-tenth of a second in front of the BMW of Lehto and Muller. For sure
it is a race I will remember all my life. The Bentley win at Le Mans was very special
– a special atmosphere, a special team, and a special car. Everything was fantastic.
It was Bentley's first win for over 70 years it was so special it is something I will
keep in my heart forever.

50 **Erik Carlsson** *Rally Champion*

It was, I suppose from a company point of view, winning the Monte Carlo Rally. But
by far, I most enjoyed the Liège-to-Liège Rally in which I came second twice – but it
was my privately entered car. That really gave me the most satisfaction.

51 **Patrick Carpentier** *Championship Auto Race Team driver*

Watching Nigel Mansell and Ayrton Senna in Spain in the Spanish Grand Prix
racing wheel to wheel, and nearly touching wheels, with sparks flying everywhere.
But for me it was winning the Michigan 500 last year [2001] that was a really
great feeling.

52 **Hugh Chamberlain** *Team Principal*

It was in April 1992. Against all advice I entered a Spice C2 car in the opening
round of the World Sports Car Championship at Monza. The team had no money and
no spares but it did have an enormous enthusiasm and a race car. In the race, the
car ran faultlessly, won its class and finished third overall. We went on to win our
class in every race that year, including Le Mans. Sometimes you have to ignore
common sense and follow your instinct.

53 **Marcus Chambers** *Sportscar driver*

It was about two hours before the 1939 Le Mans 24 Hour race was due to finish.
I took over the drive from Peter Clarke in the 1.5 litre HRG. It was not long before
I noticed that there was something badly wrong with the engine. It would no longer
cruise at its normal speed. I knew from previous experience that this was probably
due to oil starvation to the rocker shaft. I parked the car on the next lap up on the
grass just after Tertre Rouge corner and began to look for trouble. I found that there
was a shortage of oil to the valve rockers and after restoring the oil supply, I set
about adjusting the valve clearances.

I knew that we would finish the race now, and while I was working on the engine,
Morris-Goodall who was driving a two litre Aston Martin stopped and asked if I
wanted to send a message to our pit. I thanked him and said that I would soon be
OK. After that the engine ran well and we went on to win the 1.5 litre class,
finishing 14th in the GC at an average speed of 67.307mph. I shall always
remember "Mort" Morris-Goodall's most sporting gesture.

54 **Jock Clear** *Chief Mechanic*

Estoril 1996. Jacques Villeneuve overtaking Michael Schumacher around the *outside* of the last turn.

55 **John Cleland** *Touring Car Champion*

1995 was my best touring car year in the BTCC (British Touring Car Championship). We had ten manufacturers, only three or four Brits in the series and all the rest were world class and ex-Formula One drivers. It was the series that got huge credibility and television publicity. For me to win it with Vauxhall that year was great. The best year. I remember having great, close battles with Rikard Rydell in the Volvo and Alain Menu in the Renault, two drivers I have great respect for, and my best mate Will Hoy, who died not so long ago. He was a lovely guy who I trusted implicitly.

56 **Mark Cole** *Commentator*

The Formula One Asia feed TV commentator in Hungary. Although I raced myself for 10 years in the 1960s and 1970s, nothing matched the drama of Budapest 1999 as the race reached one of its few moments of real drama. Commentating at full flow, having ignored the queasy smells coming up from a hamburger stand directly beneath my trackside cabin, I felt a sinking feeling. Seconds later I was on the floor. The chair had collapsed, taking me, the power cables and monitor cables with it. Now I know what "flying blind" means, in the two minutes it took for my assistant to restore a normal service, the top three made their pit stops and the lead two changed. Somehow my commentary was in synch with the race order when it was all over. Beware of Hungarian folding chairs!!

57 **Mike Coombe** *Sportscar driver*

Racing in 1970 and 1971 in Villa Real, a town in Portugal situated about 50 miles inland from Porto. The circuit was eight miles long on public roads running through the town and around the outskirts. The track was lined by pavements and stone walls skirting vineyards. Across part of the circuit was a single-track railway and on Friday and Saturday practice was stopped twice to let the local train across, although on the Sunday the train did not run so the 500 kilometres Sports GT race was uninterrupted.

Part of the town section was an iron bridge across a gorge, the bridge surface being wooden sleepers which rattled when being crossed, but as the bridge was only wide enough for one vehicle you could control the cars behind. The road over the bridge led through the town between houses which opened straight onto the pavement with their occupants watching the race sitting on their doorsteps a few feet from the competing cars. The whole atmosphere of the event was marvellous with dinners, pre-and post-race parties put on by the townsfolk with scrutineering in the courtyard of a castle that overlooked the circuit. Alas, after 1971 the race lost his international status as the course was deemed too dangerous.

58 **John Cooper** *Owner Cooper Car Company*
The Mini Cooper winning the Monte Carlo Rally three times and the Cooper Climax winning the Monaco Grand Prix three times.

59 **Mike Costin** *Founder of Cosworth*
Being the first person to track test the DFV engine in the Lotus 49 Formula One car.

(60)

(60) **David Coulthard** *Formula One driver*
Winning the Macau Formula Three race in 1991. The reason is that at that time
a good lap was over two minutes and 20 seconds long which required a lot of
concentration, similar to Monaco but much longer. This stands out as even more
memorable than any of my wins in Formula One probably because it seemed such
an innocent and pure time in my career – pre-bullshit!!

(61) **Andrew Cowan** *Rally driver/Team Principal*
Winning the London to Sydney Marathon in December 1968.

62 **Colin Crabbe** *Sportscar driver*

Back in 1967 during the Reims 12 Hour sportscar race. I was driving my Ford GT40 that probably would reach 180mph down the long back straight, downhill (which was one-and-a-half miles long(!), revving at a maximum of 6800) when I was passed by David Piper. He was in, I think, a Ferrari P3 or P4, and we got into his slipstream and re-passed him. To my horror the rpm hit 7500 and the speed recorded at the track-side was 202mph! Wow, I got a terrific fright and beat the steering wheel badly as a result. We finished a respectable eighth, surprisingly, but the engine blew up the following week!

63 **Tony Crook** *Formula One driver*

I suppose it was either my first or my last race (400 races and 10 years later). So I
will mention both.

The very first race to be held in England after World War II was in 1946. It was
held at Gransden Lodge on a former Bomber Command airfield. There had been a
few sprints and hill climbs in the months before which I had competed in but this
was the very first actual race. I had always wanted to race and during the war,
whilst in the RAF, I had to drive round the runways and perimeter tracks in my
type 328 BMW.

While still in uniform I had joined Raymond Mays, father of the ERA and BRM.
He entered me for this first race and I won it! Thus becoming the first winner in the

UK since the war. How proud I was! After that for the next 10 years races, sprints, long-distance races followed almost every weekend. In these days we didn't just appear every fortnight as now. In 1954 for instance I entered 60 races in one season! My last race was as memorable as my first, for a different reason. My first had been a winner, my last a crash! It was the end of the 1955 Goodwood 9 Hour race and, in the dark, a Ferrari in front of my Cooper Bristol lost its oil. I spun on it and was unavoidably rammed by Stirling Moss. Stirling was just behind me and could do nothing about it. He was winning his class and so was also eliminated. I was hospitalised but when I regained consciousness the biggest bunch of flowers was from Stirling Moss. I always remember those flowers and his absolute sportsmanship, more even than the racing. How friendly we were in those days.

64 **Christiano da Matta** *Formula One driver/Championship Auto Race Team Champion*
Winning the CART Championship and racing in Formula One with Toyota.

65 **Alan de Cadenet** *Sportscar driver/Commentator*

It was at the 1971 Targa Florio in Sicily. The front and right hand wheel on my Lola sportscar broke a stub axle, came through the bodywork and hit me on the head at 180mph. I was knocked out cold. The car hit a wall, the seat belt sheered off and I was thrown out of the car which continued down the road and caught fire. It was burned out totally. They all thought I was dead. So did I because I woke up to see bright, blinding lights, trumpets sounding and I could see the ground disappearing away from me. I remember thinking, God, you've killed yourself, but I felt quite happy because at least I was going to heaven! It wouldn't have been any joy to see earth, tree roots and worms – definitely going the wrong way!!! In fact, I had regained consciousness at the exact moment a stretcher bearing a helicopter sent by the military was taking off. The pupils of my eyes were jammed up open (bright lights), the blades sounded like trumpets and of course the ground was disappearing away from me. This was the only accident I have had at this time and, from that day to this, it's all been a huge bonus!

66 **Baron Toulo de Graffenried** *Formula One driver*

Winning the British Grand Prix in 1949 at Silverstone circuit.

Yannick Dalmas *Formula One driver/Le Mans winner*
Driving across the finish line in Le Mans 1995 in a McLaren Formula One GTR for
my third Le Mans victory. In 1999, I was also fortunate enough to join the elite
group of drivers who have won Le Mans four times.

Derek Daly *Formula One driver*
The Grand Prix of Monaco, 1980. I got a good start from 12th place on the grid and
as I approached the braking point for the first corner, I looked over to see where
Patrese was positioned. While I focused on Patrese, Giacomelli in the Alfa jumped on
the brakes right in front of me. I did not see him hard on the brakes in time, and hit
his left rear wheel. The impact sent my car high into the air and into a series of
cartwheels. After landing on Giacomelli, Alain Prost and my own team mate Jean-
Pierre Jarier, I was running in about sixth place, but had no wheels left!! This
incident became one of the most used pieces of video ever in Formula One.

My other most memorable moment was qualifying tenth for the British Grand
Prix in my Ensign next to James Hunt. There were so many followers, fans, and
family there. It was my dream come true. The car was probably one of the easiest
cars I have ever driven. In the race it was good also until the rear wheel fell off. I
think it was at Paddock bend and about 40 laps in. This race at Brands Hatch for me
was the foundation of my racing career, and the Grand Prix at Brands Hatch was
such a special event. I had raced Formula Three there and this was just a special and
memorable day for me.

69 **Neil Dangerfield** *Saloon Car driver*

My triumph at Goodwood on 10th June 1961 in the Marque race for road-going sportscars. My Triumph TR3 was found to have lost compression on one cylinder a couple of days before the event and looked like being a non-starter. A few of the usual competitors, notably Bob Staples and Bill McCowen, were otherwise engaged at Le Mans that weekend. Results counted towards the season-long Freddie Dixon Trophy and I needed points badly so there was nothing to be lost by going. In practice, Kostos Pateras (AC Bristol) was just over three seconds a lap quicker but somehow I was next.

In those days the Marque race featured a Le Mans tight start with cars parked end on to the pits and drivers on the other side of the road. When the flag dropped I got away first with Kostos closing fast at Woodcote corner on lap one. He spun. The rest of the field scattered in all directions giving my sick car breathing space. By lap nine he was back on my tail, and spun again! Never was I more pleased to see the chequered flag at the end of the tenth lap. Goodwood was always my favourite track.

70 **Colin Davis** *Formula One driver*

The 13th April 1958. The occasion of the Trofeo Shell at Monza for sports prototypes under two-litre capacity. The favourite was a single works entered Ferrari. I was entered by the Maserati brothers with their one-and-a-half litre Osca. It was my first drive at Monza, not a circuit at which to make mistakes. It poured and poured with rain and I was also rather tired, my nearby hotel being on the main Monza tram route with the last rattler at midnight and the first around 3.00 am. In the hours between, a thin wall away, an anonymous couple in the next bedroom were providing astonishingly loud approval of passion, and insatiability. Viva l'Italia! But please let me get a wink of sleep!

On race day, the rain increased and I decided to let the Ferrari set the pace. My idea was to slipstream behind until the end of the very fast back straight and later pass under braking at the Curva Parabolica. I left the braking just that little bit too late. A bad mistake. The Osca slid off the outside of the bend into the muddy grass verge and then further on, right to the top of the old earth parapet which followed the contours of the Curva Parabolica (no gravel run-offs or tyre walls in those days!).

The top of the parapet was flat and the long suffering Osca consented to being driven along it, then down the slope to rejoin the circuit and the race. This was that sheer good luck which successful generals and racing drivers need. The second piece of good luck was that later, catching up with the Ferrari, it suffered a problem and ended up somewhere between the old Curva Grande and Lesmo. The Osca won the race and put up fastest lap. It completed a third success after my first two races at the end of the previous season for the Maserati brothers, the Sicilian Coppa d'Oro at Syracuse and a race at Rome.

Lucky 13th April 1958 became my first passport to an annual contract with Ernesto, Bindo and Ettore Maserati.

As most retired racing drivers know, some of the many collectors of autographs and memorabilia can be, shall I say, a mixed blessing. But occasionally, humour – intended or unintended – finds its way of creeping in. Recently, a stalwart enthusiast obviously battling with a difficult foreign language wrote to me:

" . . . *from this time I attract attention to your name, Mr Davies, how did you enthuse countless people by your courageous driving style by the roadside?"*

By the roadside? Ouch! Forget the flattery, forget the hyperstate . . . But that roadside bit perhaps does have a point. At least on that occasion, 40 odd years ago.

71 Richard Dean *Sportscar driver*

Winning outright in a GT2 Viper at Silverstone in the rain. My team mate, Kurt Luby, and I qualified seventh overall in the dry, behind McLaren's, Lister's, GT1 Porsche's, etc, etc. When the rain started half an hour before the race, we felt we had a chance to finish in the top three overall and win the GT2 class. The rain was very heavy and I started the race, handing over to Kurt in second place, Kurt passed Julian Bailey when the race restarted after a "pace car" period. We held on over the last 10 minutes to score a narrow but very memorable winner overall.

72 Tom Delaney *Motor racing elder statesman and driver*

My first races at Brooklands in the 1930s where I did quite well. I got quite a few second places and some first places but to me it was all equally exciting wherever I finished. In 1931 I got pole position for the first time in the Irish Grand Prix at Phoenix Park. I held the lead for about 250 miles then I had rather a long pit stop unfortunately and lost my place. An Alfa that had been following me took over the lead, but he had a long pit stop and some bad luck and lost out too. That was a very exciting race.

I remember racing at Donington Park when it first opened I even managed to beat Richard Seaman, in my small Lea-Francis. I've always raced with the same Lea-Francis car. My father bought me the car soon after I left school. He used to race in his day and he was anxious that one of the family should continue in the sport. This car that he bought me is the same car that won the TT race in 1928 with Kaye Don driving. Unfortunately the war came along and I took up flying. I really didn't know what to do with the car and so I reluctantly sold it. It was bought by a doctor who was later put in charge of a hospital in Aden and he took the car with him. He did hill climbs and sand racing with it. I managed to track him down though through the hospitals – his sons were both doctors too and I managed to get his address. We subsequently had a meeting and discussed him selling the car back to me but he was not too keen. A week or two after the meeting I had a letter from him saying that he couldn't sleep that night and I was to have the car back. And I've had it ever since.

I'm not sure how long the car and I were parted but it was throughout the war years and a little time after as I was in charge of the family engineering business. As a member of the British Racing Drivers' Club I was asked to serve on the board. It was with people like Lord Howe. We were therefore responsible for organising most of the early races after World War II. I have raced this car ever since. I particularly like going back to Ireland where I had my first pole position. I also like racing at Silverstone and Donington Park. I used to drive to the circuits in the Lea-Francis, race and then drive home. We do not do this now as the traffic is so great and the car would simply over heat in the long queues. I therefore have to have a transporter for the car.

Norman Dewis *Sportscar and test driver*
Driving a Jaguar D-type in the 1955 Le Mans 24 Hour race when Levagh, the French driver in a works Mercedes, crashed into the crowd of spectators killing 85 onlookers including himself. One never forgets moments like this.

74 **Keith Douglas** *Writer*

It was 11th June 1955 at the Le Mans 24 Hour race. Motor racing's bleakest day compounded by the refusal of the organisers to abandon the race. The facts were that the race had been running for two hours and 28 minutes when an accident occurred in the most densely packed area opposite the pits. Despite the utter carnage with over 85 people killed and well over 100 injured, there was little panic other than in the immediate incident areas. So packed with spectators (said to total some 500,000) was the area that most were isolated from the accident and were unaware of the gravity of the situation. Had the race been stopped chaos would have ensued as spectators in the immediate area of the accident would have suddenly become aware of the accident and either have moved to that area or, even worse, flooded to the exits to get away, and inevitably prevented easy access to and from the circuit.

As I was present during this blackest day in motor racing history, I witnessed the authorities' valiant attempt to succour the injured and, where possible, evacuate the area. Every conceivable form of transport was commanded and my abiding memory is of casualties being taken away to Le Mans hospital on the backs of open lorries and vans. If the race had been stopped many of the injured would undoubtedly have not survived. Whoever made the decision was right and deserving of commendation. On returning to Elmdon Airport on the Sunday evening I will never forget the crowds of relatives on the tarmac searching for the faces of their loved ones, and only then did we realise the enormity of the disaster and the worry for our families at home. Although many of us tried to telephone home after the accident there was a total breakdown of communications out of the circuit so we were effectively cut off from the outside world.

The impact on the motor-racing world was far reaching with Switzerland banning circuit racing and every circuit throughout the world taking a hard look at its safety procedures.

Tony Dron *Sportscar driver*

Was to win in the Eifel Klassik on the old Nürburgring in a Ferrari 330 LMB in
1996. However, *the* most memorable was chauffeuring Innes Ireland across London
for lunch in 1967.

76 Keith Duckworth *Founder of Cosworth*

It was a postscript to Trevor Taylor's story when he won a hundred bottles of champagne at Reims. [See page 232.] I remember him bringing the champagne to the greasy spoon cafe near to the factory. There we were drinking this wonderful champagne out of thick mugs, I shall always remember this as it all seemed so out of place.

77 Geoff Duke *World Champion motorcycle rider*

In 1950, winning the Senior TT race in the Isle of Man for the first time.

(78) Once is happenstance, twice is coincidence, but three times is bloody stupid!

78 **Peter Dumbreck** *Sportscar driver*

Le Mans, 1999. I was on my fifth lap of the circuit driving around 200mph when the front of my car began to rise and I saw the sky. My first thought was of the trees on the other side of the track and how I didn't want to hit them! Then I woke up in the ambulance!

79 **Mike Earle** *Team Principal*

If I have to identify a particularly special day out of my motor racing career after nearly 30 years, it would have to be 24th September 1989. It was when, with the Moneytron Onyx Formula One car, we had finally graduated into Formula One after many years in Formula Two and Formula 3000. Some of them successful and championship winning, some of them not so successful.

We turned up at Estoril and pre-qualified, which was always a lottery in those days, and started from twelfth spot on the grid with Stefan Johansson driving. We had a good race and managed to stick in somewhere around seventh or eight place for most of the race until we moved up to fifth, when other teams stopped to replace tyres. Probably because we were not sure we could do the job sufficiently quickly, but maybe because we identified that the cars that didn't stop only gained any time for a period of two or three laps, we decided to go the whole distance on one set of tyres.

Our fifth place was improved considerably when Nigel Mansell and Ayrton Senna had their much publicised coming together and both went off. And there we were in our first year of Formula One on the podium amid such luminaries as Ferrari and McLaren. A truly memorable day, and one I wouldn't have missed.

Ben Edwards *Commentator*

The start of my first ever Formula Ford race in the wet at Brands Hatch. I pulled away gently as the lights changed, all looking good, then changed up into second gear and floored the throttle. The car immediately turned sharp left and deposited me, nose-cone first, into the Armco barrier directly below the well-filled grandstand. I was several shades of red beneath the crash helmet. Perhaps I should have realised then that I would be better off behind the microphone rather than behind the steering wheel.

Guy Edwards *Formula One driver*

Mike Hailwood had broken his ankles and I had broken my wrists. In 1975 we were both recovering at the Farnham Park Rehabilitation Centre. The food was awful. So, together we could drive a car – me operating the pedals and Mike the steering and gear lever. We sneaked out and operating the car in this way, made our way to a restaurant and had a slap-up meal. However, on the way back the police stopped us as Mike had his plastered legs leaning out of the window. Much discussion followed as to the merits of the two incapable people combining forces to drive the vehicle. The police were winning the argument, took out their summons books and asked for his name, which he gave them. Immediately, all was forgiven, autographs provided and off we went.

82 **Vic Elford** *Formula One driver*

The 1968 Targa Florio. I was driving a Porsche 907. My team-mate was Umberto Maglioli. On the first lap after leaving the village driving up the mountain chasing second, something happened. The wheel came loose and the tyre burst. I got out and found the centre lock had undone itself and the tyre had burst. The spectators nearby lifted up the car and I fitted the space saver spare wheel. I made it back to the pits to change the tyre losing a total of 16 minutes all in all. I drove eight of the eleven laps and lapped consistently inside the course record taking 67 seconds off Muller's previous lap record. With two laps to go I pulled away and recorded one of Porsche's most famous victories. My race time was eight minutes quicker than the 907's winning time of the year before. Porsche normally create a poster for the following year's race showing a picture of a car. In 1969 the poster showed a picture of me instead of the car.

83 **Teo Fabi** *Formula One driver*

I haven't had too many. The day I won the pole position at the Indianapolis 500 was a special moment for me. It did make a difference to my career.

Jack Fairman *Formula One driver*
Winning the 1000 kilometre race at the Nürburgring in 1958 with the Aston Martin.
This was the first British car to win at the 12-mile circuit in the Eiffel mountains
against full teams of Ferrari, Maserati and Porsche. No other British cars apart
from the Aston Martin competed.

Geoff Farmer *Historic racing car driver*
It was at Zandvoort, Holland in August 1992 with my Theodore historic Formula
One. We'd had a very fraught practice with clutch problems. With five minutes still
to go I did it three fast laps, every one quicker than the previous, and each one good
enough for pole position. I and my team were elated having won pole from John
Surtees' driver (one Teddy Pilette, an ex-Grand Prix driver) but when John himself
made the effort to seek me out, shake me firmly by hand, and to glowingly
congratulate me on my driving, the word PRIDE took on a whole new meaning. So
thank you John Surtees – you are indeed a BIG man.

84

85

86 **Adrián Fernández** *Indy Racing League driver*
Any time I have won. So for me it's all my wins.

87 **Ralph Firman** *Formula One driver*
Being given the opportunity of racing in Formula One with the Jordan team.

88 **Giancarlo Fisichella** *Formula One driver*
Second Monaco [1998] and Canada [1999].

89 **John Fitzpatrick** *Sportscar driver*

Winning the 1000 kilometre race at Brands Hatch in 1983 in a Porsche 956. Derek Warwick and I beat the factory teams. It was really wet and that was quite something, beating the Rothman's Porsches. Derek was a good driver to drive with. He was fast and good with the car. Also in 1980 at Le Mans when we led for 14 or 15 hours. We finished fifth in the end, but it was a good and exciting race.

There have been several similar exciting things that have given me pleasure but those two do stand out to be very memorable for me.

90 Ian Flux *Sportscar driver*

In June 1989 at the Willhire 25 Hour driving with Ian Taylor and Ricky Fagan (Mercedes Cosworth 2.3). We had been introduced to Tom Ryan who looked after the Silk Cut Jaguar drivers.

Tom reckoned we needed the special glucose anti-dehydration drinks to help us through the race. For the first 15 hours he was absolutely right. You had to drink a one-and-a-half litre measure about 20 minutes before you got into the car which would gradually dissolve in your body during the two-and-a-quarter hour stint. It all works perfectly while you are at racing speeds!!!

I took over from Ian Taylor at 3.45 am. At 3.55 am the fog descended. It was that foggy for the next one-and-a-half hours while we drove round in a crocodile behind the pace car. At about 4.15 am I realised I had a major problem between my legs!!! I was not at racing speed and I had one-and-a-half litres of fluid in my bladder!!! I got on the radio and asked what I could do. I couldn't come into the pits — we would lose our lead. I couldn't stop on the circuit in case somebody ran into the car. In the end, there was only one thing to do. It took three laps because every bump I hit turned the tap off. And what was originally reasonably warm became distinctly cold over the next one-and-a-quarter hours. Not very pleasant but it was the only course of action.

I had not told Ricky Fagan what had gone on. He commented on the radio that considering Flux had been behind the pace car for nearly two hours, we couldn't believe how much sweating I had done. In fact, it had made the seat damp!!! I told him on the rostrum after we had won the race. He then saw the funny side of it. I have only used good old-fashioned water ever since!!! The tip is to make sure you have enough water that your urine is crystal clear. At that point you have had enough and your body will be fine for two hours of hot sweat in a race car. Or, of course, you can always wear a nappy!!!

91 **Paul Frere** *Formula One driver/Writer*

When I went to report on the 1956 Belgian Grand Prix. I had taken part in it for the last four years and had won many races on the old, super fast Spa-Francorchamps circuit. But this time I would be going to the Grand Prix to report on it as a journalist. Being part of the Jaguar works team in sportscar racing, I had made no arrangements to drive in Formula One. I did not have the time for both.

I was just about to leave Brussels to report on the first day of the Grand Prix practice when the telephone rang. At the other end was Eraldo Sculati, the Ferrari team manager: "Luigi Musso broke a wrist last week at the Nürburgring and Mr Ferrari wants you to drive his car in the Grand Prix!" "Sorry, that's impossible," was my answer. "I have not driven a Formula One car for exactly one year. (I drove a Ferrari into fourth place in the 1955 Grand Prix.) I am too much out of practice and don't want to make a fool of myself in front of the Belgian public."

In fact, I had finished second in the Reims 12 Hour race sharing a D-type Jaguar with Mike Hawthorn a few weeks earlier. But a Formula One car is different, more nerve-wracking, and I really feared not to be up to the task.

When I got to the circuit on the first day of practice, Sculati again tried to persuade me to drive but I stuck to my decision although I was very anxious to try the car. It was the Ferrari version of the Lancia D50 – the best Formula One car around that year – and my impressions would make a good article. "Yes, by all means, do a few laps," said Scarlatti and went off.

It really was a super car, the finest racing car I had ever driven. I felt quite happy with it, Sculati was very persuasive and I finally gave in. There was another practice session on Saturday and I would take part in it.

In qualifying, nobody managed to challenge Fangio who also drove a Ferrari –
not even Moss in a works Maserati. Obviously my fears not to be competitive would
be justified: I only qualified in midfield. But fortunately for me, in the race itself
which went over 500 kilometres (the Grand Prix distance in those times) started in a
drizzle and I had always been rather good in such conditions. As the race proceeded,
I felt more and more confident and overtook Trintignant and Schell, both driving
Vanwalls, who had qualified better than me, then Jean Behra's Maserati, while
Castelloti and Fangio, both in Ferraris, fell by the wayside and Moss who had a
problem, had to take over Perdisa's Maserati. Just before half-distance, the rain
stopped, the road slowly dried and with the finish in my sight, only my team mate
Peter Collins was still ahead of me. The order remained unchanged as we raced over
the chequered flag when I learned that I had done the third fastest time in the race.

So the journalist who had come to report on the Grand Prix finished up with six
world championship points in his pocket – and no regrets.

Avec les compliments de

PAUL FRÈRE

92 **Nanni Galli** *Formula One driver*

I have one or two but it's very difficult to remember. One was when I was at Le Mans with the two-litre Alfa Romeo T33. I was racing through the night, it was very wet, it was the Porsche in front of me and then in the morning I was first. The battery and the alternator blew up on me and I had to stop. But I think I could have won.

The next one was when I drove for Ferrari in Formula One. I was with Jacky Ickx in a 312B. The car ran quite well but the mechanic didn't want to change the engine. The engine had done a race before with Clay Regazzoni but was losing about 50 horsepower. Anyhow they did not change the engine and I finished in front of Ickx. Very good!

93

Howden Ganley *Formula One driver*
Don't mention the Maki!! [The Maki was a Japanese Formula One car which
Howden practised for the 1974 German Grand Prix. Unfortunately the suspension
broke and the car crashed leaving Howden with severe ankle and foot injuries. These
injuries resulted in his retirement from Grand Prix racing.]

Derek Gardner *Designer*

It was the finish of the United States Grand Prix at Watkins Glen in October 1971.
It had been a memorable year for the Tyrrell team. Jackie Stewart was already the
new world champion and the "new man," François Cevert, had been following his
every move. It was now the stated ambition of François to win a championship race
and I believed that he could do this having qualified fifth fastest for the grid.

Jackie led from the start but was soon in trouble with his tyres. François, who had
a slightly different set up on his car, was clearly faster and was waved past on lap
eight. For a time, François was hounded by Jacky Ickx in his Ferrari but the Ferrari
was sidelined by the alternator falling off. As he took the chequered flag François
raised both arms in exuberance, the first Frenchman to win a Grand Prix for
15 years. As a memento, François had a golden medallion struck that depicts
this unique event.

Frank Gardner *Formula One driver*

It is a thought that has been with me for many years where I never wished to be the
quickest in my chosen sport, I just wished to be the oldest.

96 **Mike Gascoigne** *Designer*

While I was at Tyrrell under Harvey Postlewaite, he and I used to drive over to Belgium for the Spa race each year; Harvey in his Ferrari Daytona and me in a 308 GT4. One year I drove round the old Spa circuit while Harvey related doing the same many years before as a passenger with Innes Ireland and pointing out many of the famous landmarks on the old circuit. A great memory of Harvey who sadly passed away this year [1999]. A great loss to motorsport and engineering.

97 **Graham Gauld** *Writer*

How could I forget the day Jim Clark asked me for driving advice? Now that was a day to remember and one never to forget. However, it was not quite as dramatic as it might appear.

The year was 1958 and we had driven north from Edinburgh to the Aberdeenshire circuit of Crimond with Jim driving an empty Thames van with a trailer and the Border Reivers at D-type Jaguar on the back. He was to race this car and Ian Scott Watson's Porsche 1600 Super. At the circuit, during untimed practice, Jim had a problem. It is well known he sometimes had difficulty making up his mind and this was such a time. He tried the Porsche using the normal Michelin X tyres he had used on his journey to the circuit. Then he tried the car with Dunlop racing tyres. He then asked if I would go round the circuit with him as he couldn't decide which wheels to use in the race. The clerk of the course agreed too – things were relaxed in those days – and we headed out onto the circuit first with the Xs which wobbled and swayed as they did on a Porsche in those days. Then we went out on the Dunlop racers. There was no choice, "Use the racers," I said. He did, and he won the race. Now that's something to remember. He never asked my advice again!

98 **Oliver Gavin** *Sportscar driver*

I think it was winning the British Formula Three Championship at Thruxton. It was really a memorable moment because it had been a tight championship. I was racing Ralph Firman all the way through the year. He had quite a big lead midway through the season then I started getting the points back. I won a few races on the trot, he had a few bad races and that set things up for Thruxton. It worked out that whoever finished in front of the other would win the championship. I had a particularly good weekend and he was having a bad one. I had qualified third. I got a good start but it turned into a mess after the first couple of corners and I ended up on the grass. I thought I was going to throw it all away but I managed to hold it together. As the race turned out, it was quite simple. For last few laps you're thinking something can go wrong. But coming across the line for the last time all the boys were up there, over the wall, screaming and shouting.

It was a particularly good feeling because we had beaten the Paul Stewart racing team that had dominated the Formula Three Championship for five or six years. In fact, it was the first time they had ever been beaten. It was a great achievement and the team were delighted.

Contrary to popular belief my most memorable moment was certainly not taking the chequered flag in a Grand Prix driving the safety car! I much prefer racing.

99 **Peter Gayden** *Racing driver*

Winning my first British Formula Three championship race. The race was at Mallory Park and my car was a year-old Brabham BT18. I had had some car melody [a term used in the 1960s for strange engine noises] during practice and I stuttered round for three laps just to qualify which put me on the back of the grid. The track was slippery from earlier rain and I remember making a really good start and passing several cars around the outside of Gerrards. Thereafter I drove as fast as possible with no real hope of success. I kept passing other cars and on the last lap dived inside a slower car at the hairpin. Coming through the Devil's Elbow I was very surprised to see the chequered flag. I had won. Later I learned the car I passed on the penultimate corner had led the race from the start! One of my special moments in a much enjoyed motor sport career.

100 **Marc Gene** *Formula One driver*

My fifth place in a Grand Prix for the Minardi team. Purely because for a very small team like Minardi, points are very precious.

101 **Peter Gethin** *Formula One driver*

It was after crashing very heavily opposite the pits at Brands Hatch in a Formula 5000 race. I ran across to the pit counter to see if my then girlfriend, now my wife, was OK and not in a state of total shock. Upon asking her if she was OK and not worried about my life, she calmly told me that I was far too selfish to hurt myself and was not worried in the least! I think she still feels the same to this day.

(101)

102 **Andrew Gilbert-Scott** *Sportscar driver*

In 1991, I was driving the number one – Jaguar – with Jan Lammers and Patrick
Tambay at Le Mans. I remember only too well my first experience of the circuit as it
was very dark, wet and foggy. I was going down Mulsanne thinking how fast it was,
eyes out on stalks. Looking for the famous kink, I glanced down at the speed to see
180mph and realised I needed it to be doing 250 through the corner. Later we were
leading when we had to change the gearbox at 4.00 am. I was the first to drive with
the new box fitted. The number one mechanic came to me and said, "Take it easy for
a lap to make sure it's safe." I took it out of the pits and, as I entered the Mulsanne,
I thought what is taking it easy – 220 or 240? Let's face it, if it's not OK, it's not
going to make much difference when you hit the trees!!! So I put my foot down and
we climbed back to finish fourth.

103 **Fred Goddard** *Team Principal*

The time I first had pole position. I will never forget the feeling of being right at the front almost as if the lights are there just for you!

104 **Jose-Froilan Gonzalez** *Formula One driver*

One of my most memorable moments in motor racing was Silverstone! [In 1951, Gonzalez won the British Grand Prix at Silverstone for Ferrari, the first Grand Prix victory for the now famous racing marque.]

105 **Jean-Marc Gounon** *Formula One driver*

It's very difficult in a long career to choose one moment. But I should say it must be the year of the Ferrari F40 [1996]. It was very nice because we had a bloody incredible car, very fast, but very difficult to drive, and for me total concentration was required, a very difficult thing to control. For sure a most incredible car to drive.

The world waited with bated breath, would they do it, would they do it at last?
Would New Labour give the 'Bernie" back to Bernie?

106 **Stuart Graham** *Motorcycle and racing driver*

Winning the 1974 RAC Tourist Trophy race, thus achieving a unique double having won an Isle of Man TT in 1967 during my motorcycle racing career. Winning the RAC TT again in 1975 was an added bonus.

107 **Andy Green** *Land Speed Record holder*

The day we took Thrust SSC supersonic for the first time. When I rolled up to a stop at the end of that run, three minutes and 13 miles from the start, the recovery crew were already celebrating. But the timekeepers hadn't announced the speed yet. How did the crew know we'd been successful? Then I realised. They had heard the sonic boom – the first ever from a land vehicle. We had done it!

108 **Ken Gregory** *Team Manager*

The day I flew to Stuttgart in late 1954 to meet the legendary Alfred Neubauer, team manager of the equally legendary Mercedes racing team.

A telegram had arrived at the flat I shared with Stirling Moss literally minutes before Stirling was due to leave to fly to New York to compete in the North American Mountain Rally for the Rootes Group. Neubauer wanted to know if Stirling was engaged for the 1955 season and invited me as his manager to visit the factory and discuss terms for Stirling to join the team. In the heat of the moment, Stirling suggested I should wire back and say we were not interested. After Stirling's father Alfred and I had taken Stirling to the airport, we decided the opportunity was just too great and I wired Neubauer to confirm the meeting.

Just meeting Neubauer was memorable. The terms of the contract were even more memorable, and Stirling's year with the team in 1955 probably the greatest year ever. The lunch that followed with the great man and an interpreter would have been more memorable but for the generosity of the host. On arrival, the lady of the house produced a silver tray with 12 glasses of white wine, all of which we consumed. Then through the interpreter Neubuer asked me, "Which of the four wines would you like with your lunch?"

109 **Nicky Grist** *Rally co-driver*

My first Safari Rally, after only two events with Colin McRae and having driven a near-perfect event, we had an alternator failure on the penultimate section. After some 20 minutes we managed to limp into service, repair the fault and complete the last section for victory!!!

110 **Dan Gurney Formula** *One driver*
It was breaking down at the Nürburgring 1967 Formula One Grand Prix with
a third of a second lead and three laps remaining!

111 **Carl Haas** *Team Principal*
There have been so many. I'm really enjoying myself here at Rockingham
[2002]. We really had some good times with Nigel Mansell in 1993.
He won some great races.

Hubert Hahne *Formula One driver*

I really have so many. Any fastest lap or driving a corner on the limit is a nice experience. To get a corner just right. When it was a record lap too, or winning, that was nice. But really driving a corner fast, on the limit, placing the car right.

Bruce Halford *Formula One driver*

Strangely enough, not winning a race or surviving a serious accident, but qualifying to race in the 1959 Monaco Grand Prix. Grand Prix races were run to the 2.5-litre formula at this time, but I entered my 1.5-litre Lotus. Only the quickest 16 in practice were going to start and at the end of three laps' practice, I ended up 16th having beaten a lot of 2.5-litre cars including some factory cars. I was also the only non-factory car on the grid. It gave me great satisfaction.

114 **Jim Hall** *Formula One driver/Constructor of Chaparral*

It was at Mosport in 1965. I had an engine failure in qualifying and that started
me clear at the back. I worked my way through the field and caught up with
Bruce McLaren about ten laps from the end. We had a real battle to the finish
and I was able to put a final pass on him about three laps from the finish. That
was a wonderful race from my standpoint, and yes, my most memorable moment
in motor racing.

115 **Tim Harvey** *Touring Car Champion*

I'm trying to think whether it was on or off the track! I think, probably, the most
emotional I have ever been in a car was the first Le Mans I did. It had been a
real struggle to get to. The team had a real problem with drivers, sponsors and
one thing or another. We had our own car and were trying to do Le Mans and the
World Sports Car Series and that was with Charles Ivy in a Porsche Tiger. We got
to Le Mans. (It was my first race there.) I started the race, did the session going
into the night, a session during the night and the session going into the morning.
We had a few drive shaft problems but managed to fix them. We were leading in
class although we had these problems and then we had to pit two or three times
more and we came out still second in class and finished in the race as well. So I
did all the best bits. To finish the race second in class with all the British marshals
waving their flags around was really the most emotional I have ever been in a car.

Neville Hay *Commentator*

The day I set fire to the commentary box at Thruxton. This was during an hour-long race and required the ingenuity of my lap scorer and myself to dowse the flames. As to why it occurred or the method used to quell the fire, I leave to your imagination. However, the cloud of steam that this produced caused us more trouble since it totally obscured our view for a short time. That no one knew of our plight I put down to the well-established fact that no one listens to the commentary anyway!

Hans Heyer *Formula One driver*

I dedicate this page to my good acquaintance and friend Ayrton Senna, the greatest driver of all time.

Walter Hayes *Designer*

There have been so many! But the one I shall never forget was the victory of the Ford GT40 at Le Mans in 1969. It was by no means the first GT40 triumph there, but the car driven by Jackie Oliver and Jacky Ickx was said to be getting too old. Jacky Ickx crossed the finishing line two seconds ahead of the second car, the closest finish, I believe, in Le Mans history.

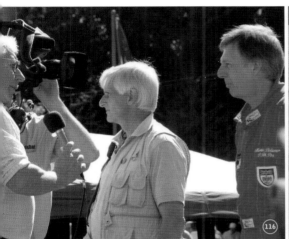

One of my most memorable moments in Motor Racing was ....

Ih widme diese Seite meinem guten Bekannten und Freund Ayrton Senna dem größte Fahrer aller Zeiten.

11. 10 99

Moments in MOTOR RACING

119 **Patrick Head** *Designer*
Alan Jones winning the 1980 French Grand Prix against strong local opposition
from Renault and Ligier. It was a drive that showed all his strong qualities as a
driver and personality.

120 **Johnny Herbert** *Formula One driver/Le Mans winner*
Winning the 1995 British Grand Prix.

121 Damon Hill *Formula One World Champion*
One of my most memorable moments in motor racing was crashing into
Michael Schumacher for the third time!

122 Phil Hill *Formula One World Champion*
When I won the World Championship in 1961.

This is one of my favourites. The British GP when Damon crashed into Michael at Priory. Damon must have had a 'Remember Adelaide' sticker on his dashboard.

123 **Roger Hill** *Mechanic*
When we came in first and second at the Nürburgring in 1973 with Jackie Stewart and François Cevert. François unfortunately was taken away from us soon after but I'm sure he would have made world championship the following year.

124 **Paddy Hopkirk** *Rally driver*
When we surprised the world by winning in the 1964 Monte Carlo Rally with a little Mini Cooper. To receive that prize, at the Monte Carlo Palace from Princess Grace, is a great memory for me.

Will Hoy *Touring Car Champion*

Competing in the Nürburgring 24 Hour for the factory Prodrive BMW team.
I started but at the end of the first lap, all 14 miles of it, I had an engine problem
so I peeled off into the pits. The very relaxed regulations meant that we could change
the now-defunct engine which the Prodrive team did in unbelievably quick time.
Within the hour, I was out on track again but only completed two-thirds of the lap
when the car ground to a halt. I eventually diagnosed a flat battery so, using my best
German, persuaded an extremely inebriated spectator to part company with his Ford
Granada heavy duty battery, one which we got over the safety fence with the help of
the marshals! With the use of the various branches from the forest, I managed to
wedge the ridiculously oversized battery into the boot. The car started and off I went
in a huge power slide to show my gratitude to the now almost horizontal spectators.
I got back to the pits but the problem was I had been gone nearly one hour and
without radio communication, the team had assumed I had retired and had packed
up the pit so when I entered the pits they were nowhere to be seen! I eventually
tracked them down and the car was returned to the track, albeit a few 14-mile laps
down. I had handed over to Jeff Allam and I borrowed the hire car and eventually
found the spectators and duly returned the battery!

David Hunt *Racing driver*

It was a major shunt I had at the Super Prix, but perhaps it wasn't as memorable for me as it was for my parents. They were having their Sunday lunch watching the race. Apparently, because I have no recollection of this, they were about to start their main course when they saw me bouncing off of Tesco's wall. It wasn't memorable for me because I lost my memory for three months as a result of the accident. It did come back to me later. That was a big shunt – the car split in two and I wasn't particularly well after it. What makes it most memorable, I'm told, is that Channel 4 did a documentary about Birmingham's famous sights and apparently there is a blue plaque or something on that Tesco's wall, near to the hole I made – they didn't ever repair it.

A memorable moment about James has got to be when he won the World Championship. Ultimately, that's the best thing he ever did. I was about 15 or 16 at the time. The race wasn't live on TV in those days so I was invited, along with the whole family, to the ITV studios to watch the live feed from Japan. Barry Gill was commentating, so it's just us and the ITV people. At the end of the race James was told that he had won the World Championship, but he didn't believe anyone. He said he was not prepared to believe anyone until all the officials had gone home, because until then they couldn't take anything away from him. After that we all went home and had a great big party.

Jacky Ickx *Formula One driver/Le Mans winner*
I have had so many wonderful memorable moments in motor racing. It has been
so good to me, I've had such a great time. I suppose really, it could be said, all my
Le Mans victories were very good.

Taki Inoue *Formula One driver*
When the course car hit me. That was at the 1995 Monaco Grand Prix. I was in
my Footwork-Hart Formula One car and the French driver, Ragnotti, was driving
the other vehicle. That's about as memorable as it gets.

129 **Jean-Pierre Jabouille** *Formula One driver*

When I won the European Formula Two Championship at Hockenheim in 1976.
It was a big fight with March, it was very important for me because I was in my
Elf 2. You see it's not always Formula One.

But in Formula One, I don't think it was my first Grand Prix of France. I think
it was the race after, I'm not sure. Anyhow, it was the one where I was fighting with
Alan Jones and I had a big problem with my left front tyre. I was in the lead but as
we came to the last corner my front tyre was finished. I thought he would catch me
so I pushed very hard and held on to win the race that was at Zeltweg. Zeltweg is
a very good track, very difficult, very quick, and I like it very much. This race I
remember as being a very, very good day.

FOR TONY JARDINE

130 **Tony Jardine** *Commentator*

When I was rallying my Talbot Sunbeam for the first time on a big national rally
in South Wales, sponsored by Chingford Fruit Packers. My bright idea was to carry
bags of fruit so that we could distribute the fresh produce to officials along the route.
Unfortunately the bag burst open over rough section of the stage and two big ripe
apples rolled under the brake pedal as I was careering downhill. There were two big
pieces of Port Talbot (no play on make of car) steel round rammed into the ground
acting as gateposts at the apex of the bend. I hit the brakes which only managed to
part mash the apples and not stop the car. We slammed into the post head-on and
banana'd the car. Worse was to follow. Sitting above the stage watching with
disbelief were Tony Pond and Robert Arthur who had retired their prototype Metro
6R4 a little bit further down the stage. We all sat the rest of the stage out together.
I did however offer them pieces of pre-cut and peeled apples!

131 **Jean-Pierre Jarier** *Formula One driver*

When I met Enzo Ferrari in July 1973. I spoke with him in Italian and I signed
a contract to drive his Formula One car. I was so happy.

132 Jean-Pierre Jaussaud *Le Mans winner*

Well, it's been so long. I have been racing since 1964. It's a long way and I have had so many nice cars to race: Formula Three, Formula Two, Formula One – testing but never in a race. Sportscars, of course, with two wins at Le Mans with Pironi in the Renault A442B and Rondeau in his own car. I have raced at Le Mans 13 times, also the Paris–Dakar Rally eight times. All of these are memorable moments.

133 David Jensen DJ/Team Principal

It was our first win in Formula 3000! Watching Nicholas Minassian storm to a brilliant win when he led from lights to flag at the British Grand Prix 1999. It was the most exhilarating and exciting experience of my racing life.

134 Jonny Kane Sportscar driver

It was to win the 1997 British Formula Three Championship, emulating my racing hero Ayrton Senna, and becoming the only Ulster driver to achieve this in the history of Formula Three.

135

136

135 **Nobuhiko Kawamoto** *Mechanic*

Watching Ayrton Senna, now he was really different to the others.

136 **Rupert Keegan** *Formula One driver*

Winning the Aurora Championship at Silverstone with David Kennedy knocking me off, spinning through the chicane, he went straight into the barriers – that pissed him off – but I managed to carry on and finished second.

137 **Louis Klemantaski** *Photographer*

For the 1956 motor racing season the great Enzo Ferrari had signed up my good friend Peter Collins to drive for his team. As the Mille Miglia, one of the dwindling numbers of great town-to-town races was definitely on the list, and I had some previous experience of this race for the Aston Martin teams, Ferrari thought it would be prudent to enter us for a similar race to see how we would get on with one another, spending some ten hours travelling at high speed confined to the cockpit of one of his sportscars. So he entered us for the Giro di Sicilia, a Mille Miglia type race run over ordinary roads, and the competitors being flagged off at minute intervals, our main opposition coming from Piero Taruffi in a works Maserati who was starting two minutes before us.

At the various controls and our refuelling pits along the route, we were fed with the latest positions, for which we could see that Taruffi had built up a healthy lead of six minutes and had decided that he could afford not to press his car too hard. We got this information at the last control at Messina and Peter set off, determined to make up those vital six minutes. By dint of some real Grand Prix driving Peter managed to beat Piero's time by 15 seconds. And I got a unique photograph of the winners at the chequered flag taken from the winning car as it crossed the finishing line!!!

COME ON ERNIE — YOU'VE MISSED A BIT!

FOR 'ERNIE' KNOTT

138 Ernie Knott *Signwriter*

It was in May 1949. I had started a sign writing business in Brackley trading as Enotts Sign Service. The following year I was offered work by the track manager Jimmy Brown to carry out sign work for the Silverstone circuit. I became the official sign writer to the BRDC and wrote the main scoreboards that were erected in the pits area in addition to lots of direction and entrance signs. One of my duties was to number the racing cars prior to the International Trophy meeting and at the Grand Prix plus some club meetings.

I recall attending on the grid at the start of the 1952 British Grand Prix with paint and brush in hand. Engines were started, revving and raring to go. The chief timekeeper shouted to me that he could not see the number on the wide mesh of the grille on Mike Hawthorn's Cooper Bristol and instructed me to paint another number nine on the right hand side of the nose panel. I quickly stepped into action and as I completed the number the flag was dropped and the grid swept away in a cloud of rubber. A scary moment it! The winner was Alberto Ascari in the 500 Ferrari and Mike was third having started a fourth on the grid.

136 Tom Kristensen *Le Mans winner*

Winning the 1997 24 Hours of Le Mans on my debut (including a new lap record) with Joest Porsche!

140 **Jan Lammers** *Formula One driver*
Qualifying fourth in 1984 US Grand Prix with the ATS Formula One car. It turned
out to be the closest I would ever get to the top! It is great and a privilege to be a
racing driver!

141 **Pedro Lamy** *Formula One driver*
It was probably when I first tested a Formula One car for Team Lotus, or with
sportscars of course. I won the GT2 Championship with the Viper, and my two
victories at the Nürburgring were great.

142 **Roger Lane-Nott** *British Racing Drivers' Club Secretary*
To be the Formula One Race Director in 1996 when Damon Hill became World
Champion. The last race at Suzuka was a memorable time, particularly so, as I was
in the Race Control with Herbie Blash trying to ensure everything ran smoothly. It
did and Damon became World Champion.

143 Tony Lanfranchi *Formula One driver*
Was – or is – just doing it!!!

144 Niki Lauda *Formula One World Champion*
The Lisbon race in 1984, winning the World Championship by half a point.

145 David Leslie *Touring Car driver*
Racing at Spa in a Group C2 car. My team mate in the other car had managed to spin it at the top of Eau Rouge at the beginning of the weekend and write it off. The boys back at the pits worked hard and spent a lot of time putting it back together. We were obviously told not to go out and do that again, but about ten minutes before the end of the race, I spun the car again at the top of Eau Rouge. Luckily I didn't hit anything and bought the car back in one piece. I simply didn't tell anyone. To this day they still don't know about it but I suppose they will now!

146 Les Leston *Formula One driver*
Winning my first important international race, the 1952 Luxembourg Grand Prix. In 1952, I also became the first recipient of the BRDC Richard Seaman Trophy. Forty years later, I had the pleasure of presenting it to Nigel Mansell. If I am around in 2002, I hope the BRDC may ask me to present it to the 50th winner. (I'll get my Zimmer oiled.)

147 John Lewis *Sportscar driver*

Surprisingly, not trying to buy Silverstone(!), but doing 200mph at Charlotte Motor Speedway under lights!

148 Brian Lister *Constructor*

The 1955 Empire Trophy organised by the BRDC at Oulton Park where Archie Scott Brown driving a Lister Bristol won this prestigious event. The events leading to this had all the drama of a *Boy's Own* story!

Archie Scott Brown was born in 1927. He was terribly disabled, his right hand was at all but missing and his legs and feet were malformed. Twenty-two operations in early childhood enabled him to walk but only after determined practice over a long period. By the time I met him in 1952, he was competing in club motor sport. I was so impressed with his abilities that I asked him to drive a car I had built up with a Tojeiro chassis and a JAP air-cooled engine. The combination worked so well

I decided to design and build a car carrying my name and using an MG engine. This was the first Lister and was completed ready for the 1954 season.

One of the first events we entered was the prestigious British Empire Trophy. But this race was at a different class to those races Archie had driven in hitherto. Consequently, drivers were checked before the race. Archie had already practised and achieved a very good time. However, the doctors at the circuit were amazed at the extent of his disability and he was banned from racing. This was a shattering blow to Archie who really lived for motor sport. An appeal was made for his competition licence to be restored and because of his a proven record and the way he had driven in practice at Oulton, his licence was restored by June 1954.

In these few months I had built up another car with a Bristol engine, a larger and more powerful unit than the MG. This car proved to be an immediate success and for the rest of 1954 Archie scored many wins and places in both Lister MG and Lister Bristol.

One of the first races for 1955 was the British Empire Trophy. Archie was entered in the Lister Bristol and, in a drive that I can only describe as "inspired," won the race demonstrating that here was a master of motor racing who a year earlier had been banned in the same race at the same circuit. This winner caused a sensation in the sporting press and the newspapers of the day. Archie was a hero who was to become a legend. The story of Archie is told in the award-winning book *Archie and the Listers* by Robert Edwards, published by Patrick Stephens.

In 1957, I designed and produced the first Lister Jaguar which Archie drove in 14 races that year, winning 11 and breaking the lap record in practice for the race on all the circuits. One of those 11 races he won was the 1957 British Empire Trophy!

His struggle for success from what would appear to be insurmountable difficulties had been won, but the story was not to have a happy ending. On May 18th 1958, he was competing in a Lister Jaguar at Spa in Belgium, he had just been accepted by the organisers in Europe when he was fatally hurt in a racing accident. Nigel Roebuck, writing about Archie in *Autosport* magazine a few years ago, said that there was never a braver man in motor racing. Few would argue with that and *Motor Sport* magazine, in 2000, listed him 27th in a list of the 100 greatest drivers of the century.

Richard Lloyd *Sportscar driver/Team Manager*

Finishing second at Le Mans in 1985!

Freddy Loix *Rally co-driver*

My first World Championship podium in 1997 in the TAP Rally of Portugal.

Dave Luckett *Chief mechanic*

I'm tempted to choose the 1975 Race of Champions at Brands Hatch, but I think that win was more down to the skill and talent of Tom Pryce than anything else. So that moves us on to the 1977 Austrian Grand Prix.

Having tragically lost Tom a few races earlier and failing to even cross the start line in the previous race (the German Grand Prix when the car in front of Alan Jones stalled on the grid which resulted in Jones destroying the front corner of his DN8!) the team went into the weekend hoping things would improve. This unfortunately was not the case to start with! We had all sorts of problems in practice, and Alan Jones could only manage 14th on the grid. The car ground to a halt unexpectedly out on the circuit during the last lap of practice, after the DFV decided to go no further. (Back then that meant Dave James and myself taking a walk to find the car!). We did not have to go far, as it was discovered at the top of the hill. Because Formula One cars still had on-board starters then, and electric at that, I got into the car and the engine fired up without hesitation.

Thinking we could drive downhill into the pits, David James climbed onto the rear wing and off we went. We were somewhat surprised to meet a pace car coming over the hill and were informed we would have to do a lap of the circuit following behind it! After rounding two or three corners, race cars, Formula Three I think, were passing us on either side on their way to the starting grid! Looking in the mirrors and seeing David James very white faced as he clung on, proved it was not the place to be at that moment!

Back in the pits, and that bit of excitement over, we started to race prep the cars. After changing "the bomb" on the DFV the cut-out problem was solved. (The same engine was utilised all weekend.) So warm-up went fine and, mainly down to Alan Jones. we found ourselves leading with ten laps to go. Those last few laps were full of emotions. History shows that Alan Jones and Shadow won their first Grand Prix. We had the thrill of the victory, sadness that we could not share that with Tom Price, and the laughter remembering the look on Dave James face in his precarious position!

152 **Peter Lumsden** *Saloon Car driver*

Driving my Lotus Elite WUU 2 in the 1000 kilometres at the Nüburgring in the early 1960s. It was a wet day. Towards the end of the race I was leading up my class and aiming not to take any undue risks when Stirling Moss, driving a GT Porsche (different class), came up to overtake as we were approaching a corner. I pulled over to let him pass and he promptly drove into the back of my car because, he said afterwards, he was going too fast and that was the only way he could slow down enough to make the corner.

153 **Perry McCarthy** *Formula One driver*

There have been so many, but one thing I've learnt is never to wave to Damon Hill during a race. We were fighting for third place in a Formula Three race at Silverstone in 1987 and I managed to overtake him coming on to the back straight. As I went to pass I couldn't resist teasing him so I waved bye-bye. In return my pal, Damon Hill, moved over on me and put me off the track!

Ed McDonough *Motor racing journalist*

Having been a keen motor racing follower since the early 1950s, I consider myself lucky to have a number of moments to choose from. I got into participation through minor events and then jumped from Formula Ford in 1972 to the World Sports Car Championship for some races in 1973. Subsequently, I did a lot more racing later: the Ring 24 Hours and three(!) 24 Hour races in 2CVs. As a journalist I have now tested many of the great racing cars and that has been terrific.

But if I had to choose a moment, it would be in the Spa 1000 Kilometres in 1973, where I was sharing Tony Goodwin's Dulon-FVC. We few Dulon drivers took a lot of stick because the Dulon-Porsche had been knocking Ferraris off the track over the last two years!

Spa was my first sportscar drive, and it was on the old circuit. Jackie Stewart said anyone who claimed to like it was lying or crazy – I'm both then. Nineteen seventy-three was the last year every Grand Prix driver was in sportscars and saloons. I was a real rank amateur in a race with Pace, Merzario, Ickx and Redman in Ferrari 312PBs; Bell, Hailwood, Ganley and Schuppan in the Mirage; Graham Hill, Amon, Pescarolo and Larousse in Matras; van Lennep, Muller, Follmer and Joest in Porsches; Stuck, Lauda and Muir in BMWs; plus all the good Chevron drivers in 2-litre cars; and Stommelen/de Adamich who I saw crash the Alfa Tipo 33-12 in practice.

My moment was well into the race at the end of the long, long Masta Straight going into Stavelot. I just caught a movement ahead of me as the Krebs/Kautz Capri rolled and caught fire. I was committed to the line but Henri Pescarolo was coming in quicker and so was he! The burning Capri was spinning on its roof and I edged to the inside as Henri came through on the very inside, and I rubbed him and removed the mirror off the Matra. Henri waved and was gone. I didn't speak to him until some 25 years later when a mutual friend brought us together. Henri reluctantly admitted remembering two things about the Dulon: it was green – and it was slow! We remain friends.

This moment just overshadows the practice when a tyre started to deflate and Pace was behind me as I hugged the wheel and held the centre of the road. He went right, then left, then past on the right on the grass, through those old fast swoops at 150mph. I apologised later and Pace said, "What?" – he never noticed it. The old circuit was unbelievable. The Dulon could do 169-and-a-half down the straight with a tailwind and the Matras came by 50mph quicker. What a place for a boy racer.

I remain on good terms with many of those guys, and with Christine Beckers too, who was in a Chevron. Somehow a race on the old Spa circuit was as special as anything you could do in racing.

Mike MacDowel *Formula One driver/Hillclimb Champion*

Driving the works Cooper Climax Formula Two car as a team mate of Jack Brabham in the Prix de Paris race at Montlhéry race circuit near Paris in 1957. Part of the original banked track was used, and it was my very first experience of racing on quite a steeply banked track and sensing the downward G-force as one drove round to that part of the circuit. The difficulty was coming off the banking on to the conventional circuit, one had to "lay off" the steering as the angle of the banking reduced, to ensure we stayed on the road! Jack won; I was a clear second. What a memorable day!

156 **Allan McNish** *Formula One driver/Le Mans winner*

Standing on the podium after winning the Le Mans 24 Hour with Porsche in 1998. On the marque's 50th anniversary after a gruelling fight with Toyota, Laurent Aiello, Stefan Ortelli and myself climbed to the top step of the podium. With 50,000 people standing below, the pit-lane and main straight was engulfed and I could still identify specific people in the crowd, the people that made it possible. The noise, view and emotion was thankfully captured in a photograph taken by Stefan Ortelli with a small corner camera showing three enormous grins with the Le Mans crowd as a backdrop. A most memorable moment.

157 **Colin McRae** *World Rally Champion*
Crossing the flying finish on the 1995 RAC rally. It was my first World
Championship win or stop the second one hasn't happened yet but 2000 could
be the year!

158 **Jimmy McRae** *Rally driver*
Stopping Malcolm Wilson from being British Rally Champion in the 1980s –
joking!! I think winning my first Circuit of Ireland Rally and also my first British
Rally Championship.

159 **Tommi Mäkinen** *World Rally Champion*
Becoming World Rally Champion in 1999 for the fourth consecutive year.

160 Darren Manning *Indy Racing League driver*
Signing the contract with the BAR Formula One team as a test driver, that was a big dream come true. Also, signing the contract for my first Indy Car race, on my home track at Rockingham, is right up there with my memorable moments.

161 Nigel Mansell *Formula One World Champion/Indycar Champion*
Racing with Ayrton wheel to wheel, in Hungary and Barcelona, being "the Best."

162 Lord March, Duke of Richmond & Gordon *Founder of Goodwood Festival of Speed and Goodwood Revival*
Seeing Dan Gurney tackle the Goodwood Hill in the Eagle-Weslake.

(163) **Innes Marlow** *Privateer Rally driver*

So many memories, so little space! Watching or competing? If you love rallying like I do, there are a few hundred vying for selection. So for rallying fans first: Colin in the 6R4 on the McRae Stages, awesome!; Bertie in the lanes of Ulster; Gwyndaf using the full width of the Welsh forests; and the sight of a Celica sliding through a water splash on a crisp November morning, all noise and steam!!! And from inside the car, making it to any finish ramp with all corners attached. Driving the Duns lanes faster than my skill should allow. Retiring in the last forest on the RAC, that's memorable.

But better than any of these: after three years of failing, we put our self-prepared, very Group N, Mitsubishi into the top 40 on the RAC. It was more than just a rally in 1999 as my Dad was very ill with cancer and my mum, caring for him, was unable to be at Cheltenham to greet us. Because of that, my most memorable moment in motorsport was when we returned home to Hampshire and I gave my Dad my medal.

Andrew Marriott *Commentator*

Starring as the hapless interviewer in the famous *It'll Be Alright On the Night* British TV programme. Unknown to both myself and my producer, a camera was rolling on my attempts to interview Mario Andretti at the Swedish Grand Prix in 1978 although our camera was mainly on the pit road in pieces. I didn't hear any of the hilarious production chat. Several months later I received a letter and an offer of £50 to appear in the new programme. At that time no one knew what Denis Norden the presenter was up to! But don't believe everything. The interview did happen, was recorded in London and went to air as the tease at the beginning of *World of Sport*. I've done thousands of interviews since and had some good cock-ups but everyone remembers this!

165 **Tony Marsh** *Formula One driver*

When I drove a BRM at Shelsley Walsh for the first time. I had only sat in the car for the first time in the morning of practice, no proper seat fitting or anything, and during the course of weekend I broke the record four times. I think that was in 1961. The car I had was the two-and-half litre BRM. After that I felt obliged to buy it. It was in the August that I bought it and I kept it for all the next season. After that I bought the new Interim BRM but that only had to a four-cylinder Climax engine in it, and they then sold me one of the BRM V8 engines. Unfortunately I had a load of trouble and I found I just couldn't cope with it. So I decided to give up circuit racing and stick to the hills.

166 **Gerry Marshall** *Saloon Car Champion*

Was the 24 Hour race at Spa Francorchamps in 1977. My co-driver was Australian legend Peter Brock, and my little 2.3 litre Firenze battled through squall and rain to secure overall class win and the team prize. The car hadn't turned a wheel before official practice. Truly memorable and inspiring against the might of Ford, Opel, BMW, Alfa Romeo et al.

Nick Mason *Pink Floyd Drummer/Historic racing driver*
Being taught at the old Nürburgring circuit by Derek Bell in 1981 before a 1000 kilometre race. After we had finished, the rented 3 series BMW from Hertz had more illuminated warning lights than a Christmas tree.

Jochen Mass *Formula One driver*
Still being around in 2005 and racing.

Alain Menu *Touring Car Champion*
Seeing Niki Lauda finishing fourth at Monza in 1976 (I was 13 years old then!), only six weeks after his life-threatening accident at the Nürburgring. I was very impressed. Lauda was a hero of mine at that time (and has been ever since).

And, for me, winning the 1997 British Touring Car Championship at my first ever championship.

*—ALAIN MENU, RUNNER UP, BTCC CHAMPIONSHIP, 1994, 1995 & 1996!

Alain Menu was walking away with the BTCC, the 'Boring Touring Car Championship.'

Arturo Merzario

170 **Arturo Merzario** *Formula One driver*
[At the time of sending his memorable moment, Merzario had lost his trademark
hat, hence the sketch. Fortunately, he was later reunited with it as the photo shows.]

171 **John Miles** *Formula One driver*
Not Formula One, but coming out of retirement to share the Wiggins Teape Group 2
Cologne Capri with Australian Brian Muir and winning the 1973 6 Hour touring car
race at Paul Ricard, beating the works Capris and BMWs in the process. I think
Jackie Stewart and the works Ford Team were a bit miffed! There was no bank at
Ricard. On that same night, we stuffed 88,000 French francs in cash into a suitcase
and left for home, which was very nice!

172 **Philip Mills** *Rally co-driver*
Winning the 1997 British Rally Championship on the last stage of the Manx
International Rally.

173 **Lord Montague of Beaulieu** *Owner of the National Motor Museum at Beaulieu*
Although I'm not a racing driver, I have taken part in various vintage races. My first
race was at Brands Hatch and I won the Edwardian Handicap in a Prince Henry
Vauxhall 1914. A wise and older man told me it was bad luck to win your very first
race as it's likely you'll never win another. He was right!!!!

173 **Mort Morris-Goodall** *Sportscar driver*
The 24 Hour race at Le Mans which was, in fact, two races in one. The main race,
won by the car covering the greatest distance, and the Cup Biennial for cars which
had qualified the year before. I was driving a two-litre Aston Martin in the 1937
race and had qualified in the 1935 race driving a 1500-litre Aston. (There had been
no race in 1936 due to a rail strike.) The race started as usual at 4.00 pm on
Saturday and finished at 4.00 pm on Sunday and at about 1.00 pm on Sunday
afternoon Robert Hitchins (my co-driver) and I were well in the lead for the Cup
Biennial (better known as the Rudge-Whitworth Cup). Then disaster struck. One of
the valves dropped into its cylinder. Robert managed to get the car to the pits and we
did what we could do there. The race regulations required that, to be classed as a
finisher, cars had to complete a last lap in a given time and to cross the finishing line
after four o'clock under their own power. I set out at about 3.30 pm to try to do one
lap in half-an-hour on three cylinders. The car sounded awful and each time I got to

a corner I wondered if it would be best to change gear, and thus increase revs or chug round in top. At last the finishing line came in sight and I waited until I was sure that a four o'clock had struck. (Had I have crossed before, it would have meant doing another lap and that was definitely not on.) At last, I crossed the line to learn that we had won. That was a race I shall never forget.

Another memorable moment was, there used to be an annual event at Hyers near Toulon. A 12 Hour race and I was co-driver in Nigel Mann's Aston Martin DB3. We had decided to drive three-hour spells with Nigel starting, which left me to do the last spell. At 5.00 pm Nigel came in and I took over. The car was running beautifully but after an hour or so I started to get clutch slip. We had expected this and had tried to get a replacement from the factory but they had been unable to supply it for some reason. I tried everything even crossing my legs and using my right foot on the clutch pedal. That worked until the brake pedal needed attention and obviously I was heading for a monumental shunt if I kept that up. I called into the pits and asked them to fill two buckets with water and I would pay them at another visit in due course! This I did on the next lap and there were the buckets. I stopped and plunged my feet in. Oh! Blessed relief. But of course it didn't last and soon things were as bad as ever. Never was I so glad to see the chequered flag. We finished sixth overall and fourth in our class which wasn't bad considering, but I had to wear a bedroom slipper on my left foot for the next four or five weeks!

175 **Sir Stirling Moss** *Mr Motor Racing*
Winning the Mille Miglia in 1955.

176 **Ivan Muller** *Touring Car Champion/Ice Racing Champion*
There have been many great moments as I started racing when I was ten years old
and I'm in my thirties now. The first one that comes to my mind was the 24 Hour
race – that was ice racing – which I started some eight years ago. The race was the
Chamonix 24 Hour race when we completely burned the car. I burned myself in the
face and some parts of my body. One week later we were back racing with the car
repaired. All the guys had done a fantastic job of repairing it, rebuilding a complete
car in three days! We won the race and that was one of many in a long series that
gave us the Andros Trophy.

(177) **Gordon Murray** *Designer*

Winning my first Grand Prix in South Africa (my home country) in 1974 –
Brabham's first win for many years.

(178) **Matt Neal** *Touring Car Champion*

It's got to be Donington in 1999. Driving with Dynamics and leading the race,
stalling in the pits, all this live on TV, a proper fairy-tale I suppose. I had to pinch
myself really. I was convinced we could do it, but when we had done it, I needed to
have a reality check to understand that we really had done it. What was really nice
about it was all the big names of British Touring cars were still in the championship,
Menu, Rydell, Muller, everyone was in there, Jimmy [James Thompson], you could
have a fair old scrap with them. It was good fun. And of course taking a big cheque
off Alan Gow.

179 **Steve Neal** *Saloon Car driver*

It was having Guy Edwards off at Oulton Park. That gave me more pleasure than anything. I remember he was in a little lightweight club racer, and Cooper's had sent us there to do some national event. We were running these two heavyweight cars, John Rhodes and I. Guy out-qualified us up by miles. I must admit it was very early in his racing career in his little Mini Cooper. He was on pole and whacked over to the left to take a fast sweeping line through Old Hall, leaving a big gap down the inside, I came up on the inside and did what Matt did to O'Neill. Unfortunately, Guy's car ended up on its roof up the embankment. He got out of his car and hurled abuse at me. We became friends many years later, though that really was a good laugh.

180 **Tiff Needell** *Sportscar driver/Commentator*

Standing on the famous Le Mans balcony to receive the acclaim and trophies for finishing third in the 1990 24 Hour race. It was the last event before the historic and nostalgic pit complex was flattened to be replaced by the new concrete monstrosity, so it was all the more memorable to have stood where so many of my heroes had stood. The works Jaguar teams that had finished first and second had moved off and the all British crew of our private Porsche 962 were greeted by a sea of Union Jack flags. Magic memories.

179

180

181 **Ed Nelson** *Saloon Car driver*

It was in my early days of motor racing. Never having won a race I went to Brands
Hatch for a handicap race. I was driving a standard E-type Jaguar prepared by
Dickie Protheroe. When the grid places were published, according to the handicap
rules, I was to be last on the grid. I waited for that starter in trepidation, watching
him, looking at his stopwatch, moving row by row, from the front to the rear,
starting row by row by the fall of the flag. Soon it was my turn, the flag fell and off
I went at great speed – backwards! However, I did win the race, the first of many of
my racing career.

182 **Adrian Newey** *Designer*

At Magny-Cours in 1991. A local motorcycle dealer had foolishly provided a pair
of Suzuki 1100s for the drivers to use over the weekend, Patrick Head and myself
commandeered them (in the interests of the drivers' safety you understand).

The paddock at Magny-Cours had the motor homes grouped round to form a

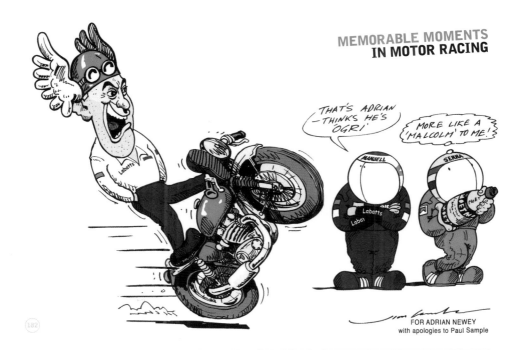

THAT'S ADRIAN — THINKS HE'S OGRI

MORE LIKE A 'MALCOLM' TO ME!

FOR ADRIAN NEWEY
with apologies to Paul Sample

little courtyard with the Williams, Camel and mechanic catering coaches forming a square. The bike was parked in one corner so when it came time to leave I thought I would give it a quick wheelie across the square, which went fine except the Camel caravan was coming up fast. A golden rule is get the front wheel back down before breaking but I didn't. The bike was buried in the side of the Camel awning with me lying in tatters beside it. As I stood out up I thought, "Where has everyone having dinner at Camel gone?" Slowly they surfaced from under the tables covered in red wine! Frank Williams gave me a ribbing for damaging a team uniform whilst the mechanics cheered. Very embarrassing.

Richard Noble *Land Speed Record holder*
Watching Andy Green and Thrust SSC break the sound barrier twice on October 15th 1997. We all saw history made that day!

184 **Steve O'Rourke** *Sportscar driver*
Building my own car, the EMKA Aston Martin, entering it for Le Mans in 1985 and leading the race for the first hour. After numerous problems we finished 11th overall, which wasn't bad for a little team from Surrey.

185 **Jackie Oliver** *Formula One driver/Le Mans winner*
Leading my first British Grand Prix at Brands Hatch in 1968 from the first lap in a Gold Leaf Lotus 49B.

186 **Stéphane Ortelli** *Le Mans winner*
On top of the 1998 Le Mans 24 Hour podium. Sharing my best victory with
Laurent Aiello and Scottish Allan McNish. Using a single-use camera shooting
spectators, team members and ourselves to capture the moment!

187 **Count Stephen Ouvaroff** *Racing driver*
My close second place to the then future World Champion Jimmy Clark at the
International Formula Junior race at Solitude, Germany on 24th July 1960.

188 **Arthur Owen** *Racing driver/Jazz musician*
The day I saw my first Grand Prix. It was around the streets of St Helier, Jersey.
Probably the last race of this kind to be held in the world. All the great racing
drivers were there. I got to know Prince Bira of Thailand during his visit. To watch
the actual race was for me a great moment. Strangely enough I did not have much
interest in motor racing, but after seeing the race I became very interested and
progressed from sand racing on the beach in Jersey to the Italian Grand Prix at
Monza, Italy and other major events.

189 **Jonathan Palmer** *Formula One driver*
Racing in the 1000 kilometre sportscar race at Monza in a Porsche 956 in (I think!)
1985. As I approached the Lesmo corners, a huge tree was blown down across the
track due to gales. So after three hours of racing, the track was blocked. Hans Stuck
screeched to a halt in the Rothmans 956 and jumped out, shouting at me to try to
help and move 200 tons of tree out of the way! Even Stuck's adrenaline was not
enough!

190 **Olivier Panis** *Formula One driver*
My best memory is when I won in Monaco in 1996 because I remember that the
whole country, the French people, were so happy.

191 **Tim Parnell** *Formula One driver/Team Manager*
It was as team manager of BRM when we won the Monaco Grand Prix in 1972 with
Jean-Pierre Beltoise as our driver.

192 **Riccardo Patrese** *Formula One driver*
Winning my first Formula One Grand Prix in Monte Carlo 1982.

193 **Win Percy** *Sportscar driver*
During practice for the James Hardy 1000 race at Bathurst in Australia. I lost
control of the car and crashed heavily into the wall. Common sense told me to get
out of the car and climb over the Armco barrier into the safety of the public area,
but what I had not allowed for was that I had written off one of their beloved
Holdens and, even worse, it was co-driven by one of their home-grown heroes,
Allan Grice. What these Aussies were going to do to this Pommie driver is not only
unprintable but it would have also been extremely painful. So I climbed back over
the Armco and sat by the car until the red flags came out to stop at the session.

194 **Henri Pescarolo** *Formula One driver/Le Mans winner/Constructor*
Well it so difficult to find just one. It could be my third place at Monte Carlo in
the Monaco Grand Prix in the Matra or it could be winning Le Mans in a Matra
with Graham Hill. Actually the most memorable would be winning with Graham Hill.

Roy Pierpoint *Saloon Car Champion*

After some thirty-odd years, being asked to take part in this charity autograph book.

Teddy Pilette *Formula One driver*

My story is funny but true. I was participating in a long-distance race at Villareal, driving a Lola T70. The weather was very hot. It was my normal practice to add glycerine to the cooling system of my car when driving in hot conditions, as when mixed with water it increased the boiling point and allowed the car to run better without overheating. My mechanics tried to buy the glycerine at the local chemists but without success. After pondering awhile we decided to drain all the water from the cooling system and fill it with wine. It worked!! We won the race too.

David Piper *Formula One driver*

It was in April 1967 at Silverstone when Formula One drivers still drove sportscars. I had a memorable race with Denny Hulme at the Daily Express Trophy. It was both political and technical; political because it involved Ferrari versus Ford. I had spent the winter making new magnesium wheels to replace the Borrani wire wheels to enable us to use Goodyear tubeless tyres, and the regulations required keeping the track original, which I had achieved. At scrutineering before the race, the Fords were all thrown out because their track was too wide. The Secretary of the BRDC and John Wyer of Ford came and asked me not to protest (in 46 years of racing I have never protested) otherwise they would not have a race, but I thought it grossly unfair and manipulative. I was furious and this made me even more determined to beat them! [Although the Ford cars were thrown out because of technical irregularities, they could race if other competitors unanimously allowed them to, and no one protested].

I put the Ferrari LM on pole but could not quite take Abbey flat. Fax, my mechanic, and I added a spoiler on the tail, which was the first time this had been done on an LM and we hoped it would work as there was not another practice session to try it. Luckily it did and at the start I managed to outdrag Denny Hulme and the rest of the field and take Abbey flat, much to my delight, and this enabled me to lead from start to finish and set a new lap record!

It was a good day for Ferrari as my dear friend Mike Parkes won the Formula One race later that day in his works car and as he was arriving in his plane he could see my green Ferrari in the lead and was one of the first to congratulate me.

Nelson Piquet *Formula One World Champion*

My first championship in 1981 was very good, when I won in Dallas.
It was very huge and I was not on my best day, but everything worked out
alright. One of the best days of my life.

Emanuele Pirro *Formula One driver/Le Mans winner*
I think it was my first win at Le Mans in 2000. I think it was much better because from zero to one is a big step. The second one in 2001 had an enormous feeling for me because we had lost Michele Alboreto so it was a very intense race, he was part of our team. The third in 2002 had an incredible meaning because with three weeks to go we had to change the drivers' line-up. So really it was a good reason to win at all my three Le Mans races.

Antonio Pizzonia *Formula One driver*
My test for Benetton in the year 2000.

Andy Priaulx *European Touring Car Champion/Hillclimb Champion*
Winning 13 out of 13 races in the 1999 season.

Peter Proctor *Sportscar driver*

The 1964 Le Mans race with the Sunbeam Tiger. We were about 12 hours into
the event (this would make it about 4 o'clock in the morning) and the car blew up.
It was as I was coming past the pits. I had just come out of White House corner,
driving flat-out. In those days there was no pit counter like there is today. There were
the pit garages, the pit road and the track. The track and the pit road were
continuous lanes. To separate the track from the pit road was just a single white line,
you were not supposed to cross this white line and if one did, it was "the guillotine,"
you're out of the race. The French were really concerned that no one would cross this
white line. Now the engine blew up. With this particular car, the Sunbeam Tiger,
some may know that the engine is shoe-horned into the engine compartment, and the
steering column is all worked out on knuckle joints to get past the engine. The engine
blew up in such a way that the metal jammed all these knuckle joints. This meant
I could not move the steering wheel at all. I suppose when the engine blew I was
doing about 150 miles an hour, while fiercely putting the brakes on but there was
nothing I could do about the steering. The car consequently drifted over to the right.
Whilst drifting and breaking the car crossed over the white line and as I was
travelling, I was coming closer and closer to the pit garages themselves. Fortunately
cars that were refuelling in the pit lane happened to be at the early end of the pit
lane as I was heading towards the latter end. I ultimately hit the pit garage wall and
scraped all the side of the car before coming to halt. The Chief Course Marshal ran
up to me and said, "Pierre, you are in terrible trouble. You have crossed the white
line. You are in bloody serious trouble and now you must move the car." So I
suggested that he got into the car to steer while we pushed. He got into the car, we
pushed and he shouted, "The car, it will not steer." So I said him, "That is why
I parked the f-f-f-f-flipping thing here."

Dieter Quester *Formula One driver*
When I finished in first place at Hockenheim Formula Two Grand Prix in front of
Clay Regazzoni, after a high-speed collision with him on the last lap. It was my first
Formula Two victory!

Jean Ragnotti *Rally driver*
My life really has been rallying. At Monte Carlo and Corsica, wonderful places
like these. For me, the best was the Renault Turbo in 1981 at Monaco — the best.

Bobby Rahal *Formula One driver/Indy 500 winner/Team Owner*
The day I won the 1986 Indianapolis 500!

206 **Jo Ramirez** *Mechanic*

At the 1993 Australian Grand Prix. It was one of those days when everyone's
emotions were running high as it was Ayrton Senna's last race with McLaren as
retiring champion and Alain Prost's last race in the Williams. Both of them were
my friends with whom we at McLaren had shared the most dominant Formula One
season in 1988 winning 15 out of 16 Grand Prix; eight for Ayrton and seven with
Alain. That day in Adelaide, we were running neck and neck with Ferrari – having
had 103 Grand Prix wins, so if Ayrton were to win he would leave McLaren on a
high note and McLaren would become the most successful team of all time by
winning 104 Grand Prix. This is just how it happened with Alain finishing second
to add to the magic. Alain and Ayrton finally shook hands on the podium, thus
putting an end to their four-year feud which had begun in 1989. That evening there
was a Tina Turner concert and Tina pulled Ayrton onto the stage and sang "Simply
the Best" to him, which practically brought the house down. I will always remember
this day.

207 **Brian Redman** *Formula One driver*

After driving well over 40 years there have been many memorable moments. To pick
one out of the bag, I suppose, I could tell you about when my suspension broke on
my Cooper. I had no steering, I had no brakes, and was going 150 miles an hour.
Something like that always sticks in your mind.

Gareth Rees *Racing driver*

It is almost impossible to select only one memorable moment from a career packed full of memorable moments, but if I had to choose one it would be my first ever win. During my career I have been fortunate enough to experience some wonderful moments: winning important races; winning championships; winning awards; driving on fantastic circuits such as the old Zeltweg and Spa; taking the outright lap record at one of my favourite circuits, Oulton Park, in one of the best cars I have ever driven, the Reynard 96D Formula 3000 car; the various Formula One tests I have carried out for McLaren; some of the people I have met and worked with.

All of these were memorable, but my first win is the most memorable of all because it was that which ultimately led to everything else. It came in a Formula Ford 1600 race at Cadwell Park and I am sure that everybody else involved has long since forgotten about it. But for me, as a 17-year-old novice, it marked a key point in my development as a driver and I will never forget it.

Clay Regazzoni *Formula One driver*

The 5th September 1999 – my 60th birthday!

Anthony Reid *Touring Car driver*

Finishing in third place at Le Mans in 1990 on my first attempt. I was driving a Porsche 962 for a private Japanese team partnering with Tiff Needell and David Sears. This result helped relaunch my motor racing career.

Adrian Reynard *Designer*

In 1995 when Reynard attempted to win at the Indy 500. Jacques Villeneuve drove one of the Reynard 95I cars but was concerned about reliability. I told him that I guaranteed him the car would do 500 miles. Unfortunately he was docked two laps in the race for sporting infringements which meant he had to race for 505 miles to finish. He did. We won the race too! I was extremely worried those last five miles and so was JV. The guarantee had just expired!

David Richards *Rally co-driver/Chairman Prodrive*

I have just been reminded of an incident in 1981 involving Ari Vatanen and me when we crashed on top of Hannu Mikkola's car. I was just able to crawl and clamber out. Just another day in Ari's rallying career!

Geoff Richardson *Grand Prix driver*

It was the 1951 Daily Express Trophy meeting at Silverstone. Just as the starter's flag was about to drop the heavens opened in a massive thunderstorm. We all got going but the course was soon flooded in places. My RRA Special seemed to like the water, and I was soon in second place, having overtaken Fangio, Gerrard and others. I spun off at Copse and got going again without losing my second spot. Spun it at Abbey, I had to wait for the field to go by. I then proceeded to overtake them again and when I had got back to seventh place the race was stopped. Won by Reg Parnell, with Duncan Hamilton second.

Tony Robinson *Mechanic*

The privilege of being involved in Formula One Grand Prix racing in the 1950s. Also seeing from the pits at Nürburgring in 1957, Fangio doing battle with the Hawthorn and Collins.

Alan Rollinson *Racing driver*

Being in the company of Jim Clark, Colin Chapman and Graham Hill aboard Graham's own light aircraft on a flight from Silverstone to Heathrow in 1968.

Ben Rood *Founder of Cosworth*

Well, I suppose I could include motorcycle racing. The most vivid memory I have was actually at Brands Hatch. John Surtees was riding that day, he was on a 250cc REG. I was riding my 250 Velocette, which most people thought was quite a quick bike. Normally I could see off any REG but somehow John had changed the bike's character. John went off into the lead and I seem to remember thinking how ever am I going to pass him? I closed in on him, near Paddock, and then all of a sudden the bike drifted away from me and I ended up on the floor. I reflected later that many people had tried to overtake John Surtees but seemed to end up in the same place as I did. I thought of starting a club up for all those people who fell off their bikes as they were about to overtake John Surtees.

217 **Huub Rothengatter** *Formula One driver*
When I started in Formula One at the Canadian Grand Prix in 1984 after three
years of not driving at all, and no practice in a Formula One car before.

218 **Andy Rouse** *Touring Car Champion*
My 60th Touring Car win at Silverstone in 1992.

219 **Tony Rudd** *Designer*
It was when Graham Hill and Richie Ginther gave BRM their first one–two in the
Italian Grand Prix at Monza in September 1962 and a substantial lead in the world
championship. It was then the custom to present the winner with a large garland of

flowers and hoist his national flag while his national anthem was being played. The trophies were presented later. This was long before the days of champagne spraying on the podium. I was somewhat full of emotion, recalling that 11 years before, BRM had been booed by the same crowd, now we had very emphatically met Sir Alfred Owen's conditions for continuing to support the team. I caught Graham's eye as we both stood up for the double rendition of "God Save the Queen" for the driver and constructor. He gave me the most prodigious wink as only Graham could. I have never forgotten that moment.

Another memorable moment occurred during the Italian Grand Prix at Monza with another one–two. This time with Jackie Stewart and Graham Hill during the 1965 Italian Grand Prix. We had probably my favourite BRM, the centre exhaust type 261 and we had found a little more power. I had exhorted both drivers not to give the game away in practice, and only use the extra performance when they saw me wearing a special signallers orange waistcoat. Soon they were in formation and had destroyed the opposition: Clark, Gurney, Brabham, Surtees, and Bandini. To my horror they started to race one another. We ceased giving them pit signals, Graham had a little slide on his last lap, which ensured he came home behind Jackie who could not understand my fury, and neither could Graham. We had won by a mile hadn't we? The engines hadn't missed a beat. What was the problem?

220 **Jim Russell** *Racing driver/Owner of the Jim Russell Racing Drivers School*
When I built the Cooper Monaco and was also running the Formula Two car and
had a mechanic with one car and Ivor Bueb's mechanic with the other. But we then
went to Oulton Park for the British Empire Trophy meeting with two cars. Salvadori,
Moss, Graham Hill were all there, and I went out, won the British Empire Trophy
with a Formula Two car. There's a photo of me with Brabham and Salvadori at the
start of the sportscar race, and I won that too. So that moment really stands out.
I was also happy with what I did with the two-litre Cooper Monaco, which I got
going faster than the Formula Two cars. I got a Trophy at Snetterton for holding
five-lap records there: Formula Three, Formula Two, the Cooper Monaco with the
two litres – unlimited and outright records. Those were all big things for me.

221 **Rikard Rydell** *Touring Car Champion*
Winning at the Macau FIA World Cup in Formula Three in 1992. I have always
liked the circuit and had a good chance of winning two times before, but I finally
won in 1992 with a Japanese team, TOMS. It was the first time that a Japanese
team won, and a great race for me!

Bob Salisbury *Racing driver*

One of my most memorable moments in motor racing was the Coy's Festival in 1999. Having not raced for some 27 years, Coy's must rate as possibly the most memorable. (Can't remember any others, silly old git!) Sitting on the grid not having made a practice start, not knowing what engine revs to drop the clutch, not really knowing which way the circuit goes and saying to oneself what am I doing here!! Still another three races later in the season, and a grand total of four races in 27 years. It's good to be back.

Mike Salmon *Sportscar driver*

I have been racing for so many years now. My first race was in Scotland in 1954 with my XK120. I think I came in third. I raced on through what you would call the really dangerous period of motorsport, but for me, and I suppose for many others it would be the most satisfying and best period of motorsport. There were, what I would call, real people, and real characters, and real cars in the sport in those days. Many drivers were killed unfortunately and I too have had my scrapes. I was very badly burned at Le Mans in 1967. I was in a Ford GT40; I wouldn't wish that injury to anyone. I was in East Grinstead hospital for up to three months and the pain was so dreadful. There's always a saying in motor racing that the more you race, the more chances you've got of things going wrong. We used to run three cars in three different championships and of course you can make a mistake, or have a mechanical failing and that's that. But still I am lucky enough still to be racing. I race in a number of saloon car races and there's Goodwood, and I'm very fortunate to still be here.

224 **Mika Salo** *Formula One driver*
Racing with Ferrari in 1999.

225 **Roy Salvadori** *Formula One driver/Le Mans winner*
The last race the Aston Martin team competed in, which was the Monza Coppa
Europe in September 1963, just prior to the Formula One Grand Prix. Two GT
Project 212 cars were entered for Bianchi and myself and the strongest opposition
came from the 4 Ferrari GTOs which had been entered, the fastest being Mike
Parkes the Ferrari works driver. The race developed into a continuous battle between
Parkes and myself throughout the whole three hours of the race and very often the
lead changed two or three times in a lap of. Monza is one of the fastest European
circuits and I found it the lap speeds and concentration needed were more demanding
than anything I had previously encountered. The heat in the car was practically
unbearable and I was thankful I was a racing against Michael, who was one of the
most experienced and skilful GT racing drivers, as our cars were very often just
inches apart. Nevertheless I was able, by virtue of breaking the GT lap record at
a speed of close to 125 mph, to beat the Ferrari by a couple of car lengths after
three hours racing. It is a race I will always remember.

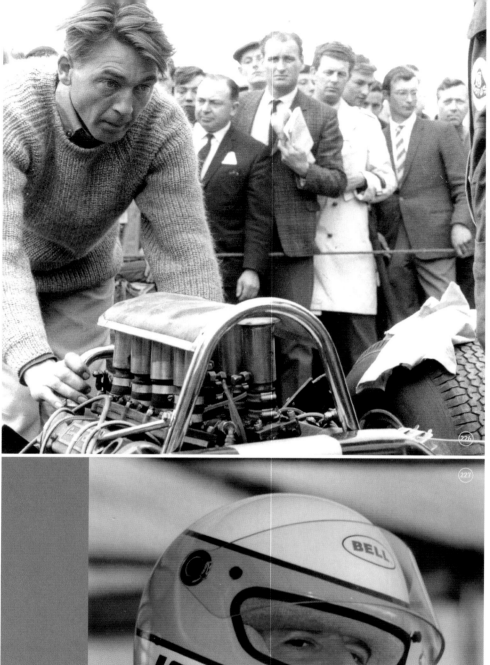

226 **Dick Scammell** *Mechanic*

It was at Spa, in Belgium. I was Jimmy Clark's mechanic. In those days we would push-start the cars. I took the car onto the grid and we were, I think, on the second row. I remember walking round the front of the car getting ready to push it back up the grid when I noticed that I was the only person standing on the grid. I thought aaarghhh! I looked up and could see the starter. (In those days, races were started by the drop of a flag.) He was about to drop the flag to start the race. I remember all the cars were revving up and wondering what will I do? Shall I try and run for the side and expect to be mown down or shall I stay where I am? I decided to just stand there and they started the race around me. I'm still here to tell the story. I remember afterwards the guard helped to push the car and get Jimmy going. When the race was over Jimmy came up to me and said, "You should have seen your face. It was a real picture!"

227 **Jody Scheckter** *Formula One World Champion*

Winning the drivers' world championship in Monza (Italy) in 1979 with Ferrari finishing first and second, my team-mate was Gilles Villeneuve. The atmosphere was unbelievable!

228 **Bernd Schneider** *German Touring Car Champion*
Racing in the DTM [German Touring Car championship] in 2001 at the Norrisring.
We were not expected to win but through a good pit strategy we managed to take
the victory.

229 **Michael Schumacher** *Formula One World Champion*
It was to be world champion with Ferrari — now it's done!

230 **Vern Schuppan** *Formula One driver*
It was in 1981. With a small budget, I purchased a four-year-old M4 McLaren Indy
Car and entered the Indy 500. The car was the only non-ground effect car to qualify
and I ended up 33rd quickest and almost got bumped from the 33-car field. I was
delighted to finish third behind Bobby Unser and Mario Andretti, especially as two
of my tyres went flat as I completed the slowdown lap. Then, following a protest
from Andretti, the win was given to Mario. Then Bobby protested. For a while
it looked as if both drivers may be excluded, making me the winner! Nevertheless,
I was thrilled to be third in my own car and team.

Peter Scott-Russell *Racing driver/Commentator*

When I had to get out of my Lotus Bristol because the engine had thrown a rod and was on fire at 140 miles per hour on the Hangar Straight at Silverstone. A sort of miracle happened – my only injury was a small burn on my left ankle. Quite a memorable moment, believe me!!

232 **Jack Sears** *Saloon Car Champion*

The European Grand Prix at Brands Hatch on 11th July 1964. I drove the Willment Cobra roadster in the Grand Touring Car support race. At the end of the first lap I was black flagged for starting on the wrong row of the grid. I restarted at about 30 seconds behind the leader Jackie Stewart in a lightweight E-type Jaguar but managed to carve my way through the field to pass him and win the race!

Cedric Selzer *Mechanic*

The Belgian Grand Prix, 1964 at Spa. The practice was dreadful. Jim Clark was way off the pace and five-and-a-half seconds slower than Dan Gurney who was on pole. This put Clark on the third row of the grid. The race distance was 284 miles (32 laps). Gurney led the race until lap 30 when he pitted for fuel. The Brabham team did not have any to hand. All fuel in those days had to be poured in from the churn. Clarke also pitted for water. The car had run so dry of water that when I unscrewed the cap there was no pressure in the system. We filled up with water and sent Jimmy on his way. Dan Gurney was also sent out. On the last lap with eight-and-a-half miles to go, the order was Graham Hill, Bruce McLaren, Dan Gurney and Jim Clark. Hill came to a standstill with the fuel pumps pumping air. If he had squeezed the bag under his legs he would have forced enough fuel into the main tanks and won. The next one to fall by the wayside was Gurney who completely ran out of fuel halfway round the circuit. This left McLaren in the lead. I went over to Pat McLaren in the next pit to congratulate her as I was sure Bruce had won. Bruce then broke down at La Source and coasted down the hill to the finish line. But Jim Clark who was following McLaren passed him with a few yards of the line and won the race. Clark, on his cooling down lap, ran out of petrol and did not realise that he had won the race. The motto of this story is "Never give up!"

234 **Carroll Shelby** *Formula One driver/Le Mans winner/Team Owner*
When I was asked by Donald Healey to drive a works car in the Panamericana, otherwise known as the Mexican Road Race in 1954. On the second day I overcooked a corner at over 100mph, lost control and flipped end over end several times. The impact was so sudden that it broke the hickory handle of the knock-off hammer, destroying my elbow. Upon observing the car I noticed that the granite kilometre marker had completely destroyed the metalled tonto cover in the passenger side. I decided the night before it was too dangerous for two people in an open vehicle in this particular race. My co-driver Roy Jackson-Moore owes his life to the fact that this decision was made by me much to his chagrin. It was hours before the ambulance came by to pick me up. However, with the help of a bottle of brandy furnished by two schoolteachers from New York and several bottles of beer by the local Indians, the wait was not as painful as it could have been!

235 **Guy Smith** *Le Mans winner*
Not surprisingly, Bentley returning to Le Mans after 71 years. A British driver in a British car with so much history, it was very emotional. With a British crowd and all the support it was really amazing. Driving any car around Le Mans is amazing but extra special when you drive a car with so much history. It takes me back to the time when Jaguar were there with the Silk Cut cars. I'm hoping that I may be able to drive the car next year and who knows I may even win.

[After Guy won Le Mans, he asked for this postscript to be included.]
Well, I'm really overwhelmed to have succeeded and won Le Mans with Bentley. It was a big risk for me taking a testing role and not racing. I never really knew if that gamble would pay off. To get the race seat was a great opportunity and then it was up to me to make the most of the opportunity. We were fortunate that the car was competitive and we had some luck. It's a big relief that we have got the job done.

236 Tommy Sopwith *Saloon Car driver*
Finishing second to Mike Hawthorn's Jaguar at the Silverstone Touring Car race in
1958, the year that he won the World Championship for Ferrari. It was fascinating
to get very close indeed to someone who was much more in control of his car than
I was, and still feel moderately safe! I do wish he was still with us.

237 Tony Southgate *Designer*
Winning the 1988 Le Mans 24 Hour race with the V12 Jaguar. Although I have
many other memorable moments this one with its massive British support is my
favourite.

238 Gordon Spice *Sportscar driver*
Winning the Spa Francorchamps 24 Hour race in 1978 in a Belga-sponsored three-
litre Ford Capri, with Teddy Pilette. It was a most satisfying win as a tyre blew out
in the early hours of Sunday morning. We were always coming from behind. The pit
stop to repair bodywork dropped us from first to eight and for the next six hours we
had to drive on the absolute limit to regain a lead. With an hour to go, a further
unscheduled pit stop left us in second place to Eddie Jordan (BMW) but the sponsor
said, "Go for it!" so we did and won by less than a minute.

231

239 **Jean Stanley** *Team Principal/Wife of Louis Stanley*

Looking back over many years of motor racing, the most noticeable difference today is the lessening of tension on race days. There used to be worries that were never put into words. Such was the race casualty rate, the only reassuring thought if there was a bad crash is that it would be somebody else, a thought that helped morale. In the meantime, lap charts kept minds active. If tragedy struck, as often happened, there was spontaneous support and comfort. Reactions were so different.

When Nina Rindt learned that her husband had died, she was calm, composed, and tear free. Her emotions were under control. Sally Courage was very distressed, clinging to the vain hope that if only Piers could be taken to the mobile hospital all would be well. Her distress was increased by the insensitive attitude of the Dutch officials. Anne Schlesser was so hysterical that the French doctor had to be physically restrained from using a straitjacket. Officials withheld the news that her husband had been burned to death. For two hours Anne and daughter were denied the facts. I sat with her throughout that long night. Doctors recommended that an ambulance journey would necessitate the use of a restraining jacket. Fortunately Guy Ligier flew her in his private plane to Paris.

On another occasion Pat Surtees experienced the agonies of suspense when John crashed. I reassured her that no one had been seriously injured, but she could not stop shaking and was in far worse shape than her husband. I had to tell another girl that the driver she was living with had been killed. Immediate reaction was not grief but how to prevent insurance policies falling into the hands of his wife. I always felt that officialdom should have been more concerned in the interest of the widows, mostly young with no financial resources or guarantees for the future. Instead they were forgotten. I recall many sad stories of acute depression, drug dependency and alcoholism. Responsibilities do not end when a driver is killed.

Happily safety campaigns have made these occasions rare, but divorce rates remain high, perhaps not surprisingly. Dewy-eyed visions of a glamorous lifestyle, endless travel to exotic countries and unbroken sunshine are soon dispersed by the reality of long airport waits, cheerless hotel rooms, living out of suitcases, climatic extremes, the realisation of the drawbacks of being married to a selfish, self-centred fellow with diminished sense of responsibility and no identity outside a cockpit. Without helmets, they are anonymous off the track. Hardly heroic, certainly not romantic. Often divorce is a godsend.

I think of one of our drivers, Jackie Oliver, with his attractive fiancée, Lynn. They had dinner with us in Monte Carlo, planning arrangements for their impending marriage. Lynn wanted the ceremony to be free of any racing involvement. Jackie had other ideas. He suggested immediately after last practice for the British Grand Prix. Lynn was far from happy. She pointed out that the wedding night would be interrupted by the bridegroom having to crawl out of bed at the crack of dawn to prepare for the race. As a compromise Lynn suggested the day after the race. Oliver's answer it was typical. "It would be too much of an anti-climax!" Needless to say, they divorced. Jackie happily remarried a more patient girl. After all, motor racing is meant to attract every type of female, including camp followers, who, as Jack Straw might acknowledge, do serve as an extra mural purpose!

Louis Stanley *Team Principal/Writer*

Recalling memorable races, one in particular stands out. Peter Gethin's victory at
a Monza in 1971. It was his only Grand Prix win but it made history.

The 3.57 miles circuit set its usual challenge with a high-speed curves and long
flat-out straights, an examination that sorted out boys from men. That year we
brought five BRMs. Jo Siffert, Peter Gethin and Howden Ganley were in the P160s
with Mark 2 engines, Helmut Marko in a P153 and a spare car. In practice Siffert
lapped 1 minute 23.95 seconds. Chris Amon took a poll position clocking 1 minute
22.40 seconds with Jackie Ickx second. Ganley was on the second row thanks to a
tow from Stewart and Peterson.

The start was sensational. Regazzoni was just ahead of Siffert as the pack hurtled
into the Curve Grand where the circuit had been narrowed. As the race pattern
settled the lead continually changed until lap 14 when Siffert and Ickx dropped back.
Stewart retired with a blown engine. Ferrari's were no longer on the list. Amon fell
back to sixth place after a nasty moment, tearing off a visor cover he also lost his
goggles.

Those opposed today to overtaking manoeuvres might be reminded of that
afternoon in Italy when the lead changed hands eight times. The field settled into two
groups. Gethin found himself in no man's land, isolated without any hope of getting
a tow. The only answer was to drive like hell. It worked. By lap 35, he was sixth,
5.6 seconds behind the leading bunch. By lap 40 the margin was cut to 4.9 seconds.
With 10 laps remaining the gap fell to 3.3 seconds. By then Gethin was with
Peterson, Cevert, Hailwood and Ganley. Slipstreaming took him into the lead on laps
52 and 53. Confident the BRM had sufficient to power, Gethin dropped back on the
penultimate lap. Everything depended on tactics at the Parabolica.

Cevert's ploy was to let Petersen through at the entrance, take a wider line and
exit first to take the lead. Peterson aimed to lead through the Parabolica, banking
on his acceleration having the edge on the Tyrrell. Gethin's challenge was discounted.
So much for theory. Gethin, brakes locking, took the BRM on the inside line. Both
Cevert and Peterson were forced out wide in parallel slides. The BRM rev limit was
10,500rpm. Gethin told me afterwards, he had nothing to lose. In high second gear,
the engine went over 11,500rpm. The engine did not blow. Gethin won by 0.01

seconds. Only 0.61 seconds covered the first four cars. It was BRM's second World Championship victory in succession. There was an additional bonus. Gethin's record-breaking winning average of 151.31mph at the wheel of a BRM became and still is the fastest in Formula One world championship races.

This victory is a reminder of those days when motor racing was a genuine sport. There was no governing body obsessed with greed and controversial deals. I'm tempted to name the two men who have bought motor racing into disrepute, but to what purpose? Sadly the clock cannot be turned back. We have one consolation. Memories never age.

241 **Ian Stewart** *Sportscar driver*
It was the awful discovery that I had eaten my whole bag of lemon drops after only four laps of Le Mans (I was driving a 1952 works Jaguar works C-type), and I wasn't just touring around, honest!

242 **Sir Jackie Stewart** *Formula One World Champion/Team Principal*
The Stewart Ford team's first Grand Prix win.

243 **Mark Stewart** *TV Producer*
When my father retired from motor racing. He said, "Paul and Mark I've got a
surprise for you." We thought: Is it a gift? Is it a present? Is it a toy? A car or a
plane? Perhaps a Dinky toy? What is it? He sat us down and we were very patient
hoping that he would pull something out of a hat any minute and then he said, "I've
retired from motor racing." What a disappointment, no toy, nothing. As a small boy
I can always remember that moment of disappointment. Not for anything to do with
motor racing but that we didn't get a present.

In terms of motor racing itself, I suppose my brother Paul's motor racing career,
and his first win. But the most satisfying is the success of the Stewart Racing team.
So much had been done in such a short space of time. When the car came home
second in the Grand Prix at Monaco, I think most people saw the images on TV, the
emotions, especially that of my father who spoke to a good many people there. It was
an incredibly good day of course, winning our first Grand Prix, the European Grand
Prix. They were wonderful days.

Paul Stewart *Racing driver/Team Principal*

I am privileged to have had several memorable moments in motor sport which have either marked me, or given me a great deal of pleasure. My most enjoyable experience in motor racing so far was in 1997 at the Monaco Grand Prix when Rubens Barrichello finished in second place in the fifth race in only our first season of Formula One. As our car crossed the finishing line behind Michael Schumacher and ahead of the other Ferrari, my father and I shared the most intense moment, filled with pride, excitement and relief. It was also unique because it could only have been experienced in this way by a father and son, but was a result of a business activity. That moment will be with me forever.

Martin Stretton *Historic racing car driver*

It was in 1977 at the old Nürburgring — best track in the world — in a works Maserati 250F, one of the most famous Grand Prix cars, taking off three times a lap, all in top gear, seven laps never to be forgotten.

Hans Stuck *Formula One driver*

When my team mate Dieter Quester crossed the finish line behind me in second place on his the roof. He crashed in the last corner and slid across the line!

John Surtees *Formula One World Champion/World Motorcycle Champion*

It was before I ever started motor racing, when in the course of one week, never having seen a motor race at all apart from when I had been with my motorcycle team to Monza where some cars were testing. I was given the opportunity of driving the works Aston Martin DBR1 sportscar that had won the 1000 kilometre of Nürburgring race with Stirling Moss driving and the World Constructors Championship winning Formula One car, the Vanwall. The venue was Goodwood, another first for me.

My life had been motor cycles and to suddenly be involved with these world-class cars and with the team managers, Reg Parnell of Aston Martin and David Yorke of Vanwall, and in the course of one week to do something like 280 laps of Goodwood circuit and be offered contracts by both teams was quite a shock to the system.

I had been as fast as anyone in those cars at Goodwood. I had my first experience of "losing it" when I became over ambitious and listening to hearsay, which I should have known better, which said that such and such a corner was "flat out." I found it wasn't and the Vanwall probably swapped ends and I gyrated through the field of barley before coming to a standstill stuffed full of it. It was, I believe, Stirling who afterwards said to me, "You didn't try to take that flat out did you?"

Well, it wasn't the start of my race career but that did come relatively shortly afterwards and I have always remembered with fondness those Goodwood days and the people who gave me those opportunities.

248 **Frank Sytner** *Touring Car Champion*
Winning my class in the BMW M3 at Silverstone in October 1988 to clinch the
overall British Touring Car Championship for the BMW/Mobil/Prodrive. A closely
fought series throughout the year, we started the race needing to win and to get
fastest lap!

249 **Alex Tagliani** *Championship Auto Race Team driver*
Without any question, my pole position in Vancouver in 2001.

250 **Patrick Tambay** *Formula One driver*
After so many races on tracks around the world to see and pass the finishing line of a
three-week Paris–Dakar Rally was more than words could describe.

Gabriele Tarquini *Formula One driver/Touring Car Champion*
It was the one point I scored in Mexico City, the only point I ever scored in Formula One racing. That was for the AGS team, just a little but a very good French team. My other memorable moment was of course in 1994 when I won the British Touring Car Championship. It is the only series I have won and I have good memories about it.

Ron Tauranac *Designer*
The French Grand Prix in July 1966 which provided us with a truly memorable weekend. The experts gave our Repco-Brabhams no chance against the Ferraris on the super-fast circuit of Reims. What a surprise we had in store for them with Jack (Brabham) coming home first and Denny (Hulme) third. To top it off, our Formula Two Brabham-Hondas with Jack and Denny driving had finished first and second in the Formula Two championship race held earlier in the day.

That evening Goodyear held a dinner in a chateau. Jack accepted the invitation on condition that it included all the team so a great evening was had by all. A transporter had to divert on his way home to collect the success bonus of 300 bottles of champagne.

253 **Mike Taylor** *Racing driver*

Being chosen by Colin Chapman to drive for Team Lotus at Le Mans with Innes
Ireland. The event itself was a bit of an anti-climax as we drove for the best part
of 18 hours in an open car in the pouring rain and were leading the index when our
rotor arm failed us. Most disappointing,

One of my most memorable moments but a devastating one was when my steering
column came unstuck at Spa Francorchamps whilst I was doing some 150 miles an
hour on the far side of the circuit. I thought I had hit oil and the car veered out to
the left plunging into an unprotected wood. This is how things were in those days.
I ended up with a broken neck and back and paralysis from the waist down and this
represented the end of my seriously competitive motoring. I was eventually
compensated for this damage by a very substantial claim against Lotus's insurers
and I suppose all's well that ends well. It was a memorable moment I could have
done without.

On a more cheerful note, winning the Brooklands Memorial Trophy was a
wonderful feeling. Finishing fourth in my first Grand Prix driving for Ken Tyrrell
at the Avus-Berlin was another joy for me and also winning the Governor's Trophy
in Nassau against such opposition as Jack Brabham, the Rodriguez brothers,
Taffy Trips, Jo Bonnier, et al., was again a great thrill. As far as I'm concerned
the whole of motor racing is a memorable event.

(254) **Simon Taylor** *Motor racing journalist/Commentator*

The final lap of the 1970 Monaco Grand Prix. Having languished midfield, Jochen Rindt suddenly came alive in his Gold Leaf Lotus 49 and put in the greatest drive of his career, which was to end in tragedy at Monza only four months later. By half-distance he was third, and with 20 laps to go he was second. But Jack Brabham's Brabham BT33 had a big lead, and Jack seemed to have the race in his pocket.

Jochen had other ideas. Breaking the lap record repeatedly, he wound in Brabham and caught him at Tabac on the final lap. He put him under tremendous pressure, but around the tight Monaco track he couldn't find a way past. With only the Gasworks Hairpin left, and a couple of back markers to lap, Brabham took a tight line, while Jochen went for the outside. But Brabham, leaving his braking too late, slithered straight on into the barriers, and Jochen swept to victory. The man with the chequered flag was so surprised he forgot to wave it. On that final desperate lap Jochen had taken 1.9 seconds off the old lap record.

255 Trevor Taylor *Racing driver*

It was when my brother Mike, who was the mechanic for Team Lotus, and I went to Cosworth workshop at Friern Barnet near London. We were to fit Keith Duckworth's latest development of the Formula Junior engine. It was to be tested at Reims, one of the fastest circuits in Europe. It was an engine to die for!

On the first day of practice in Reims, the organisers decided to award 100 bottles of champagne for the fastest lap. At the end of practice we were all of two seconds faster than the opposition, therefore securing the champagne.

On the second day of practice, it was decided to award a further 100 bottles, again for the fastest lap. Try as I might I was unable to better my first day's practice time. When discussing this with Mike Costin and Stirling Moss, Stirling pulled me to one side, saying that for 10 bottles of champagne he would find me the extra time. The suggestion was to brake, or pretend to brake late, at the end of the main back straight. This would mean disappearing down an escape road for at least 200 yards and then re-entering the circuit much faster than when taking the usual route. This found me an extra 200rpm when first passing the timekeepers box. After completion of the full circuit and again passing the timekeepers box I established a new lap record and an extra 1.5 seconds off of my previous practice time. This secured another 100 bottles of champagne, minus 10 bottles for my adviser Stirling.

There were some very intoxicated Englishman in Reims that evening! Moral to the story as quoted by Mike Costin, "You cannot buy experience. Always keep your ear to the ground."

256 Mario Theissen *BMW Motorsport Director*

The 24 Hour at Le Mans in 1999. We won the race and I think I spent most of the 24 hours on the pit wall. It was very much more rewarding than a Formula One race.

257 **Eric Thompson** *Formula One driver*
It was when Rodney Clarke of Connaught Engineering rang me in my City office and asked if I would drive a works-entered Connaught in the 1952 British Grand Prix. Despite only one practice session and a broken rev counter in the race, I came home fifth, ahead of Farina in a Ferrari.

258 **James Thompson** *Touring Car Champion*
Winning my first race in the British Touring Car Championship only a few days after my 21st birthday. It was a very memorable moment and something that always put a smile on my face.

259 **Sam Tingle** *Racing driver*
Being able to compete with the best in the Formula One championship, Brabham-Repco in 1968, and still drive the same car at Goodwood in 2001.

260 **Desmond Titterington** *Formula One driver*

Joining the Mercedes team in Sicily for the 1955 Targa Florio sportscar race.
We were to spend a fortnight learning the 45-mile lap, of which we had to do 13
laps and for Collins, Fitch and myself to get to experience the car, of which we
only had two for final training purposes. To learn the treacherous and slippery
mountainous roads, we graduated from 220 saloons to 190 SL sports and then to the
gull-wing 300 SLR sports cars before being entrusted to test out the training race
cars! It was during this learning fortnight that we often had to double up as both
driver and passenger, useful because the roads were open in the farming community
and only closed on race day!

I therefore accompanied Fangio for three laps and, while he spoke no English,
he nevertheless cautioned me about five special spots where a mistake could mean
"curtains" – his hand drawn across his throat said it all! The next occasion was with
Stirling Moss who pointed out the exact identical spots, accompanied with words of
warning (great minds think alike) but not quite with the same force as a Fangio's
decapitation gesture!

What a memorable experience! Two weeks with the all-conquering Mercedes team
headed by Ulenhaut and Neubauer and a team of 30 mechanics, etc, and with drivers
of the calibre of Fangio, Kling, Moss and Collins, and John Fitch as my co-driver.
To have had this opportunity of sitting as a passenger and learning so much from two
of the greatest drivers in the world was a highlight of my racing career. A steep
learning curve, I'll say!

I was wrong with this one too. It wasn't Mika they were sticking pins into, it was Eddie!

261 **Jean Todt** *Ferrari Team Director*
Ferrari's Manufacturers Formula One World Championship in 1999.

John Tojeiro *Constructor*

When Fangio achieved 100mph in practice (100mph lap). In 1958 I had three cars entered for Le Mans with which I had been associated. One Tojeiro three-litre Jaguar, entered by Ecurie Ecosse, a prototype AC Bristol, which won its class, and one Tojeiro 1100 Climax.

263 **Roy Topp** *Mechanic*

My involvement in motor racing started in 1971. I joined the Tyrrell Racing
Organisation and helped with the building of the first Tyrrell Formula One Grand Prix
car, Tyrrell 001. After that I became a mechanic on the cars driven by Jackie Stewart.
I was fortunate to be mechanic on Jackie's car when he won the World Championships
in 1971 and 1973. For this I owe a lot to Ken Tyrrell for giving me the chance and
Roger Hill who was chief mechanic from whom I learnt a lot about working on, and
the preparation of, Formula One racing cars. There are two races that I remember
stand out of the many memorable races which I worked as a mechanic.

Firstly, when Jackie won the Spanish Grand Prix at Montjuich Park in 1971.
It was Jackie's first win in a Tyrrell, it was his first win for a year and the first win
as mechanic for me. I felt very emotional. One of the first things Jackie said when
he got out of the car was, "It must have been the mirrors." At the very last moment
before the race cars left the workshop for Spain, we fitted the mirrors on long stalks.

The other race which is very memorable is when Paul Stewart, Jackie's eldest
son, won at Cadwell Park in the British Formula Ford 2000 championship. He drove
a fantastic race made it look easy leading from start to finish. It reminded me of
some of the great races that Jackie had won.

264 **Tony Trimmer** *Formula One driver*

Winning the Formula Three race at Monaco in 1970. Despite having driven in
Formula One many times, one of the highlights of my racing career was winning
the prestigious Grand Prix supporting Formula Three race in 1970 and becoming the
only English driver to achieve this. The memories of going out that night in Monaco
to bars and clubs with no charge anywhere and my hotel owner giving me a suite
overlooking the sea are still very vivid.

267

265 **Maurice Trintignant** *Formula One driver*

Racing in Argentina in 1955. The Lancia D50s had quite a lot of trouble but they were fast in practice. Ascari was second and Gonzalez was quickest with 625. It was a very, very hot day, the track was melting, it was terrible. Ascari was in front, but he crashed. I don't know why. Then Fangio led Moss until Moss stopped too. They tried to take him to hospital for heat stroke, but he ran away and got back into the other Mercedes! I think Fangio was the only one not to stop and share with another driver. My car started down the grid and then the engine went. Then I shared one car with Farina and Gonzalez and another car with a Farina and Maglioli. So really I finished second and third and I drove three cars in that race. Then I won at Monaco, the race when Ascari went into the water. These were both great races for me. [Translated by Ed McDonough]

266 **Jarno Trulli** *Formula One driver*

The 1999 European Grand Prix, the first Formula One podium of my life, second.

267 **Darren Turner** *Sportscar driver*

My first experience of a Grand Prix car at Silverstone in March 1997. It was a completely surreal event for me, seeing the McLaren with my name on it, managing to exit the pits without stalling, cruising down the pit lane with no idea what to expect when I hit the track. Accelerating on to the track and not being able to look down until I reached the braking area for Becketts, such was the force of the acceleration, stealing a quick look down at the dashboard between Stowe and Vale, and before I knew what had happened, I was at Vale and going onto the grass. The sheer alien nature of the whole day, never to be forgotten!

268 **Michael Turner** *Artist*

The Indianapolis 500 of 1966. Following Jim Clark's win at Indianapolis in 1965, and with the prospect of several entries from the Grand Prix world in 1966, I made my way across the Atlantic to have a look at the famous American oval which had hitherto been only of passing interest. I found the whole scene and razzmatazz that surrounded the event fascinating and felt privileged to be a small part of the invasion from the "Old Country." When the race settled down after an opening lap crash which resulted in a restart I was thrilled to realise that our three prime contestants Jimmy Clark, Graham Hill and Jackie Stewart, were all in with a chance of victory. I spent the closing stages in the pits, and could hardly believe it when Graham crossed the line to win at his first attempt. I was in the midst of a packed crowd of jostling American humanity as the victory was confirmed, and when the English national anthem was played over the public address, I was overwhelmed by a sense of patriotic pride which brought a tear to my eye.

As the crowds drifted away, I headed for the Indianapolis Speedway Inn and found Graham squashed into the corner of the tightly packed bar with a telephone to his ear. He spotted me as he put the phone down and beckoned me over. But before I had a chance to express my congratulations, he beamed with excitement and exclaimed that the horse he had backed in the Derby had won. A fact that seemed to give him as much pleasure as winning the world's richest motor race!

269 **Ken Tyrrell** *Team Owner*

The German Grand Prix at the Nürburgring in 1968. Jackie Stewart was driving my Matra Ford. We were using the original 14.189 circuit and it was a very wet weekend. The race organiser had ordered a special practice session on the race morning to allow the drivers to the places where streams of water were crossing the circuit. Jackie did not want to take part in this special practice saying it was too dangerous. For the first and fortunately the last time in my Formula One career, I insisted that he take part. Jackie led the race from start to finish winning by over four minutes from Graham Hill. A most memorable moment indeed.

270 **Kenneth Tyrrell** *Son of Ken Tyrrell*

It was a story that Dad [Ken Tyrrell] told me. It was at the Brazilian Grand Prix. Normally, Dad would walk into the circuit to his pit garage, but on this day it was raining heavily. A car pulled up alongside him and the driver offered him a lift. The driver was Michael Schumacher. Dad got into the car and as they made their way into the circuit Dad said to Michael, "I must be the luckiest team manager in Formula One having you drive for me for nothing." Michael laughingly replied at the end of the journey, "I'll now give you the bill."

271 **Al Unser, Snr** *Indy 500 winner*

I have been very fortunate in winning a lot of races. I suppose I could take any of my wins at Indianapolis, but in the end it is the win on the day that gives great satisfaction. As I've said I've been very lucky to win many races.

272 **Bobby Unser** *Indy 500 winner*

I'm not too sure of any particular race or moment but it's the wins you most remember. So I have always believed that you enjoy every win and keep something back for the times when things go wrong, remembering to listen and understand why those things have gone wrong.

273 **Jeff Uren** *Saloon Car Champion*

I think it was May 1958, the venue Silverstone, the touring car race. I had come to think that Jack Sears who was to win the championship that year was the man to beat. A Le Mans start. It seems I reached my car first and whilst there was a moment's delay buckling up the seat belts the engine fired instantly and away I went, Jack still being stationary as I went off up the straight to Copse Corner.

On passing my pit second time round I got a signal from my crew that at the end of the first lap I was an absolutely unheard of 13 seconds in the class lead. Was I excited?! My pleasure was to be short lived however for as the successive laps were reeled off so the signals indicated my lead was being reduced by between one to two seconds per lap. Soon my mirror was to be filled by works Austin A105. Somehow I was seduced into the inevitable and near to Maggots Curve. Sears went by into his regular position.

The joy turned to near misery and a feeling of resignation. I have never been one to give in but I was dangerously close on this occasion. A voice, my ego perhaps, asked what the hell I was doing. "You must go faster," it said. "If he can do it, why not you?" It was the closest I had been to my adversary so I kept good watch whilst daring to go a little deeper into each corner after him. I considered his technique and, took in his braking points, learned where he put his power on. Slowly I crept back nearer to him, worrying him at every turn. He was now having to defend each corner, needing to keep one eye on me and one ahead. Always before I had braked ever so gently at Woodcote corner, steadying the car I had supposed. I managed to stop that until I was taking a confidence lift, finding at the exit I was still in control.

Finally, feeling some considerable doubt, I managed a flat out entry for the first time and, to my utter jubilation, out I came and passed the Westminster going up the straight. Joy unknown better than anything, well almost anything! The next few laps we were to really race, swapping first place several times, but come the flag I had put my opponent far enough back to ensure a clear lead over the finishing line. Hardly able to contain myself I endured the slowdown lap before bringing the Zephyr to rest in the paddock scrutineering Bay. I must have leapt ten feet high when I got out having to let something demonstrate my exuberance. I was soon to be warmly congratulated by Jack Sears and I thanked him for the lesson, one which was to prove invaluable in the future.

274 **Nino Vacarella** *Sportscar driver*

The racing years of the sixties and the seventies were the best racing ever in the world because it was really very difficult, and very spectacular, and the cars were just fantastic. There was the Ferrari with the P2 and P3 and P4 and of course the 512. There was Porsche and Alfa Romeo. It was a fantastic world championship. The best drivers and the best cars, they all raced magnificently. We raced at magnificent circuits like Le Mans, Spa Francorchamps, the Nürburgring and Monza. Today, I think Formula One is not that very spectacular or fantastic. There's not too much overtaking, the drivers they don't really drive and are not so fantastic as we were.

275 **Jimmy Vasser** *Indy 500 winner*

Winning the US 500 in 1996, I suppose.

276 Jacques Villeneuve *Formula One World Champion/Indy 500 winner*
Winning the 1995 Indy 500 from two laps down. I guess it was the Indy 505?
It is the biggest race in the world, but what made it special, was the teamwork
and the fighting to get the two laps back and it worked. It shows you should
never give up!

277 Murray Walker *Commentator*
Watching Damon Hill win the 1996 World Championship at Suzuka, Japan.
I had to say, "I have got to stop now. I've got a lump in my throat." And I had!

278 **Rob Walker** *Team Owner*

Since watching my first motor race when I was a small boy, 75 years ago, I have had many memorable moments, but recently at Goodwood I was asked to say a few words on the same subject in front of 80,000 spectators. I chose the following story.

During my Formula One racing days, Ferrari were always our chief rivals, and the team to beat. In 1959 Stirling Moss was driving for me, and in September we took part in the Italian Grand Prix at Monza in our undersized Cooper. Monza is really the home of motor racing since the early 1920s. The spectators were about 120,000 Ferrari fanatics, known as the Tifosi. In practice Stirling managed to place the car in pole position.

It was the habit at Monza for the chief mechanic to push the car with his other mechanics and, accompanied by the owner, onto the grid. Ferrari always used only one mechanic to push the car to show off to the crowd how light and free the car was. For us this was easy with the tiny Cooper, and it was pushed into pole position, with me standing beside it. I felt very proud while thousands of Tifosi were howling at us! But I felt even prouder when Stirling bought the car home first ahead of a host of Ferraris and Maseratis.

Almost equalling this was when it in front of 300,000 Germans. Stirling, in my Lotus, won the 1961 German and European Grand Prix at Nürburgring, chased up by two Ferraris. It was a most moving moment when they played the national anthem and about 200 troops stationed in Germany spread the most enormous Union Jack flag across the grandstand.

279 **Andy Wallace** *Sportscar driver*

Driving down the straight at Le Mans before the chicanes were installed, and going over 240mph – IN THE DARK!! (An incredibly good feeling.)

Derek Warwick *Formula One driver*

Winning at the 1973 Spedeworth Superstock World Championship. I think the reason for this was that I had watched my father race when I was a young lad. My sole ambition in life then was to compete and win a world championship.

For the 18 months leading up to my ultimate win, I felt I had broken the mould. Drivers that had previously won were in their thirties and forties, and now I, this young 19-year-old, maybe arrogant, whipper-snapper, had started winning races to the extent that the world championship was in my grasp. This caused mayhem within the sport.

I remember the night very well. At that time the Wimbledon stadium held 20,000 plus spectators. Prior and during the race I had no nerves or anxieties at all. This could not be said of my father, who was also in the same race. He saw on the scoreboard that I had taken the lead. His nerves were so bad that he just had to pull off the track and watch from the sidelines. My nerves held until I had taken the flag and the championship. I was so nervous then I could not even undo my lap strap. Everything I had wished for and wanted to achieve had all come together in this one evening of such massive fulfilment. It was such a high point I really cannot begin to express the enormity of it.

I suppose though there was a negative side to it as well, being so young and achieving so much in my chosen sport. It was in 1975 that my circuit racing started when my uncle introduced me to Formula Ford. I don't think anything I have achieved since has surpassed that moment.

281 **Professor Syd Watkins** *Formula One Chief Medical Officer*
The 1988 Japanese Grand Prix, Ayrton Senna on pole, he stalls the car. There were
28 cars on the grid and, in the safety car, I made 29. Somehow he managed to
kickstart the car by rolling it down the hill when my car drew alongside him. He then
goes on and manages to overtake everybody, including Alain Prost, and goes on to
win the race. All that in the pouring rain too.

282 **John Watson** *Formula One driver*
The British Grand Prix at Silverstone in 1981 where I won! What made the day
so memorable though, was the involvement of the 85,000 fans present and the
realisation that "people power" is real and their power of thought, on a day when
others might have been expected to win, picked up over the last half of the race.
Following the awards presentation, I went on a lap of honour with Jacques Lafitte,
and was completely overawed by the track invasion, something I had never
experienced before and realised this was the expression of joy by the 85,000 fans.
It still raises the hair on the back of mind neck!

283 **Patrick Watts** *Touring Car driver*
Walking out of the Portland Hospital with my wife after being told that she was
pregnant after using IVF for years, the mobile then rang telling me that I was now
a works driver for Peugeot and I was to get an £80,000 salary!

284 **James Weaver** *Sportscar driver*
Driving with Hans Stuck at a circuit I had not raced on before, I asked him what
gears to use for the various corners. He replied, "Put it in fifth in case it's a fast
one!"

285 **Mark Webber** *Formula One driver*
Driving the Minardi to fifth place in my own Grand Prix in Australia. Not many
teams celebrate a fifth place but for Minardi it was like winning. For me being
in Australia was just the icing on the cake.

286 Mike Wheatley *Sportscar driver*

In 1985 when I was racing in the British Grand Prix support race at Silverstone and I was driving the CanAm BRM. I started from pole position but as soon as I got to Copse I was tapped into a spin. I had lost about half a lap on the leaders. I recovered from this and after just 18 laps not only caught up with everyone else, but won the race. I felt it was a tremendous recovery and gave me a great deal of satisfaction. I'm sure there are many other moments I could think of here. This one surely sticks in my mind, and of course it was on home soil. The BRM I was driving was a lively and wonderful piece of kit.

287 Sir John Whitmore *Sportscar driver*

Racing a Cobra. It was a 4 Hour race at Oulton Park. A 4 Hour race in a Cobra at Oulton Park is memorable in itself. This was a world sportscar championship race. It was a terrible race, things kept going wrong with the car with bits even falling off it. I even ran out of fuel on the slowing down lap, the tyres were through to the canvas. I have never been so glad to finish in my life. After taking my gloves off I found my hands were bleeding, so a very memorable experience. I suppose I could have told you about a race I had won, or racing with Jimmy Clark in the Lotus Cortina but I think this shows the not so glamorous side of motorsport.

NARA

Champagne
MOËT & CHANDON

Fondé en 1743

Best wishes.

Robin WIDDOWS
Cooper F1
1968   1996

288 **Robin Widdows** *Formula One driver*

It was at the finish of a Formula Two Grand Prix in Reims in 1969. The average lap speed was 140mph and the finish saw seven cars cross the line in one second! It was a photo finish, I was second. It was the only time that I beat Jackie Stewart, albeit by a fraction. He is still cross!!

289 **Mike Wilds** *Formula One driver*

Sitting on the grid of the 1974 United States Grand Prix. It was my first-ever Formula One race and to sit on a grid full of world-class Formula One drivers is something I will never forget!

290 **Barrie Williams** *Sportscar driver*

After more than 750 races and 40 years driving around in circles, standing on the podium at Brands Hatch after coming first in the International Europa Cup Renault Turbo Alpine race at the 1985 European Grand Prix. I was the only Brit in the race and I didn't know whether to laugh or cry as the large crowd was applauding and James Hunt and Murray Walker came and said that they had lost their voices cheering for me as I took the lead on the last lap!! It was also great fun!!

Sir Frank Williams *Team Owner*
Participating in the 1994 Grand Prix of Japan when Damon Hill in a Williams-Renault, and in pouring rain from start to finish, beat Michael Schumacher fair and square. This result put Damon up on a level point score with Michael prior to the last memorable Grand Prix in Adelaide. The Japanese race was arguably the most exciting for me in all my career to date.

Jonathan Williams *Formula One driver*
Winning the Gran Premio della Lotteria di Monza Formula Two race in 1968. It was all the more satisfying as it represented the first victory as an entrant of my old friend Frank Williams.

Desire Wilson *Formula One driver*
Driving for Ken Tyrrell at the 1981 South African a Formula One Grand Prix.

291

Justin Wilson *Formula One driver*

I think my greatest moment of my career so far was when I won the Hungarian Grand Prix Formula 3000 race in 2001. It was a perfect weekend for me and one I don't think I'll ever forget. I had been under pressure all season to score a lights-to-flag victory. By that I mean starting from pole and leading all the way, and this was the weekend that it all finally came together for me.

Even after the first lap of qualifying I knew I was going to go well. My car handled perfectly and in Formula 3000 where track time is so limited this is a big advantage. It meant I was able to spend my time extracting the most out of my car on the three sets of new tyres allowed in the rules rather than waste time setting my car up. I qualified on pole by nearly 0.7 seconds.

The Hungaroring is tight and twisty and in Formula 3000 whoever leads into the first corner is often the same guy who is leading out of the last! Another big factor is that the track is very dusty off the racing line (and sometimes on it!) and because I was at the front of the grid I would be starting on the clean side of the track. This meant that I was more concerned about Ricardo Mauricio who was third on the grid right behind me and my nearest championship rival, Mark Webber, who sat alongside me on the front row. I really needed Mark to finish out the points because a victory for me then would mean I was only one point away from winning the title. I made a good start and led into the first corner while Webber, on the dirty side, dropped to fourth. So far, so good.

After the first lap I had a three-second lead. But on lap two, I had a heart-stopping moment. I locked up under braking on the dust and only just made it through the corner. It seemed to me that the track became progressively worse as the race went on and fortunately it was not just me who found this to be true. While I worked to maintain a comfortable margin back to Mauricio, Webber had fought back up to third. But still pushing hard, he spun off with less than five laps to go. I led the rest of the way, which is easier to say than to do because when you are not under pressure for the lead it is sometimes easy to make a mistake. But I had already had one moment so perhaps I was a bit more focused than usual. It was a great feeling to be in control all weekend and come away needing only one point to win the title. It also meant that the pressure was on Mark to score at the next round at Spa Francorchamps. He really needed a win, but instead he crashed and I finished second and won the championship with a round at Monza still to run. But looking back now it was Hungary that was the turning point for me.

Malcolm Wilson *Rally driver/Team Manager*

It was as team manager of the Ford World Rally team, winning the 1999 Safari Rally with the new Ford Focus World Rally Car.

Peter Windsor *Writer*

The greatest and most memorable experience was meeting Jim Clark in 1968. It was the end of the Tasman series. He had just won the championship, and just won what was to be his last Grand Prix, the Australian Grand Prix at Sandown Park. I just sat down with him for about half an hour and we chatted. I think I was about the last person in Australia to speak with him. He has been my inspiration and driving force ever since. He epitomised what a racing driver should be and is all about and, indeed, what motor racing itself should be all about.

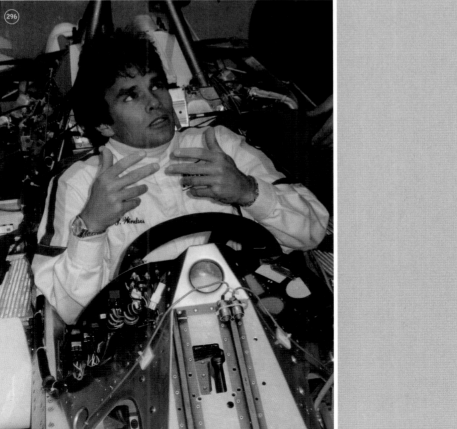

297 **Derek Wootton** *Mechanic*

My early interest in cars centred around the Austin Seven and I joined the 750 Club in the days when it used to meet at the Red Cow in Hammersmith. I was elected to the committee and got to know, amongst others, the people involved in the early success of the Lotus company. I helped Colin Chapman complete his Austin Seven special which he called the Lotus. Peter Ross was my passenger in mudplugging trials. Mike Costin was a fellow DeHavilland apprentice with Peter and was a neighbour in Harrow. Through them I met his brother Frank Costin who designed the first streamlined body for Lotus, the Mark VIII which beat the Porsches at Silverstone in 1954.

By then I was working part-time for Peter Whitehead who was racing a Jaguar, having done an apprenticeship with Ray Martin who had been preparing the Cooper Norton 500 for Stirling Moss, and then built his prototype Kieft 500 which had been designed by Ray Martin, John "Autocar" Cooper and Dean Delamont (of the RAC). David Yorke, who was Peter Whitehead's racing manager and friend was approached by Tony Vandevell using him as racing manager for the Vanwall team, and David asked me if I would like to join a company too. I said that would be fine, and I would do any job that he wanted. So I joined the Vanwall team in 1955 as transport driver, mechanic and assistant to David Yorke.

David knew that I knew Colin Chapman and Frank Costin, and noticed that I was making a lot of critical comments about the Vanwall's design and suggesting that the Lotus cars seemed to have the solutions to these problems. He asked me if I would approach Colin to design a new chassis for the Vanwall, and Frank to design a new body. This they did, and the new Vanwall used a space frame chassis and a rear suspension and wheels similar to the Lotus Mark IX sports racing car.

With Frank's new body it appeared at Silverstone in early 1956 and easily won its race in hands of Stirling Moss. This was before Stirling was signed up as a regular Vanwall team driver, and it was Harry Schell and Maurice Trintignant who were to drive the car at the Monaco Grand Prix in May. This tight street circuit was well known to exaggerate any cockpit cooling problems, and Tony Vandervell insisted that I arrange for Frank Costin to come down to Monte Carlo to supervise any additional cooling improvements to his shiny new bodywork.

Frank assured me that he would arrange everything and gave me his flight arrival time at nearby Nice airport. Unbeknown to me, Frank was prevented at the last moment from coming, and telephoned Peter Ross to go in his place, briefing him on the modifications that should be made if the drivers found the cockpit too hot.

Peter was a lowly employee of British European Airways who could travel for next to nothing if there was an empty seat on departure, but had brought his bicycle with him to save the cost of a taxi fare. Mr Vandervell told me to take the enormous chauffeur-driven Cadillac to meet Frank, and to bring him immediately to the restaurant where the "old man" would be found. I was very surprised to see not Frank but Peter get off the plane, and the chauffeur clearly did not appreciate having to load a bicycle into the back of his immaculate car.

Tony Vandervell was none too pleased at the situation and ordered Peter to be at the garage at six sharp the following morning before the first practice, ready immediately to supervise the cooling improvements. Peter set to work the next morning with the mechanics to create a slot at the base of the windscreen to allow cooling air to enter up from a high pressure point, but without spoiling the beautiful lines of the body.

Now we had to see if the modification had worked, and in the practice session both drivers came in at once, their faces were cooler, but their bodies were not. "What are you going to do?" demanded Tony Vandervell of Peter. "You are supposed to be the aerodynamics expert." Peter, who had never claimed to be anything of the sort, mumbled something about an NACA duct, but was immediately told to supervise the cutting of two huge holes in the sides of the body and rivet on a large air scoop. He protested in vain that Frank would not have liked it. "Frank is not here, get on with it." We did, and it had to be admitted that the Tony Vandervell ducts worked very well and solved the problem!

The other incident I remember well was after the Italian Grand Prix at Monza in 1957 which Tony Brooks won in a Vanwall, when Tony Vandervell noticed that one of the Maseratis driven by Willy Mairesse had a much lower seating position as the result of a new five-speed gearbox final drive unit they had designed and fitted. He decided he wanted to look at one to see if he could get any ideas for the Vanwall. We had an early 250 Maserati chassis and four-speed final drive unit back at the racing

stable at Acton. So I was summoned to his hotel, the Excelsior Gallia, probably the best hotel in Milan.

Still wearing my mechanics overalls I was directed at to the part where the "old man" was installed and giving out orders. "I want you to drive to Modena and buy me one of the new Maserati gear boxes," he said. "But they only have three of them altogether," I protested. "See what you can do," he replied. "Alright," I said, "I will go first thing tomorrow morning. They won't have got back from Monza before then." "You will go NOW," he insisted, "and be there before they arrive. There is no time to waste."

So I set off in the a Fiat 1100 we rented as a team runabout and drove slowly through the night to Modena, arriving at the Maserati factory at six o'clock in the morning. It was closed. I waited. At a quarter to eight, a cyclist arrived at the gates and unlocked them. He asked me what I wanted and I explained that I had come to see Ormer Orsi (who ran the Maserati factory) to see about buying a Maserati gearbox. He turned out to be the company secretary and invited me to wait outside Orsi's office. Orsi eventually arrived at about nine o'clock and invited me into his office. I explained that I had come on behalf of Mr Vandervell to buy a one of the five-speed gearboxes. "But we only have THREE!" he said. "Yes," I replied, "Mr Vandervell appreciates that but he only wants one of them."

Orsi looked blank, relaxed back in his chair, not knowing what to say. At that moment the phone rang, Mr Tony Vandervell was on the line asking if his man was there. The receiver was handed to me and I explained how far the conversation had reached. Orsi then asked how the gearbox would be paid for. This I related to the multi-millionaire Vandervell who exploded, "Doesn't he trust me?" I had to think quickly, if I relayed the message in those exact words the gearbox sale would be out of the window. So I said that Mr Vandervell had a very well-respected position in the motor industry and felt that his credit was good. He had also bought Maserati milling machines in the past, and was interested to buy some more for the tool room at the bearing factory. This seemed to be well received and Mr Vandervell rang off after exhorting me to do my best. Orsi then had a series of telephone conversations in Italian which I did not understand and, after some delay, I was told to go to the workshop where I would be given the gearbox.

Being slightly suspicious I wanted to be sure that it really was the new five-speed box, and fortunately caught sight of Bertocchi, the Maserati chief mechanic. I saw him at every race meeting and reckoned he would tell me the truth. Pointing at the gearbox and raising five fingers I asked him if it was what I had been told, and he confirmed it so I loaded it into the back of the Fiat 1100 and set off back to Milan.

Arriving in the hotel, still in my racing overalls, I was again directed to the bar, where Mr Vandervell asked me how I had got on. "Not too badly," I replied. He looked a bit glum and said, "Well, tell me what happened then." "Well, I've got the gearbox in the back of the car." His eyes almost popped out of his head. "Well don't leave it in the car, bring it in here." So in came the gearbox, still covered in the grime and grease from the race at Monza, and was laid on the thick carpet of the Excelsior Gallia bar for everybody to see it. I tore myself away with the gearbox as soon as possible to have a good wash and an early night before driving the transporter back to the UK in the morning.

298 **Alexander Wurz** *Formula One driver*
Driving in position one, at night, in the Le Mans 24 Hour race.

Alessandro Zanardi *Formula One driver/Indycar Champion*
It was in Cleveland in 1997 where, after being penalised and forced to last place 51 seconds behind the leader, I managed to re-pass everybody, setting the top 18 fastest laps of the race and getting Gil de Ferran with two laps to go. It gave me the most incredible win of my career!

Ricardo Zonta *Formula One driver*
Winning the 1997 Formula 3000 championship and 1998 GT sportscar championship.

MORE
MEMORABLE
MOMENTS...

MORE
MEMORABLE
MOMENTS...

MORE
MEMORABLE
MOMENTS...

MORE
MEMORABLE
MOMENTS...

MORE
MEMORABLE
MOMENTS...

Picture Credits

Moment 1	www.peteaustinphoto.co.uk
Moment 2	Ferret Fotographics
Moment 3	Kary Jiggle
Moment 4	Simon Lewis
Moment 5	BRDC Archives/www.brdc.co.uk
Moment 6	Mike Jiggle Archive
Moment 7	BRDC Archives/www.brdc.co.uk
Moment 8	Ed McDonough
Moment 9	Ferret Fotographics
Moment 10	Michael Turner
Moment 11	BRDC Archives/www.brdc.co.uk
Moment 12	Michael Turner
Moment 13	Michael Turner
Moment 14	www.peteaustinphoto.co.uk
Moment 15	Ferret Fotographics
Moment 16	Ed McDonough
Moment 17	Jim Bamber
Moment 18	Ferret Fotographics
Moment 19	Michael Turner
Moment 20	David Barzilay
Moment 21	Courtesy of Ford
Moment 22	Michael Turner
Moment 23	Ferret Fotographics
Moment 24	Simon Lewis
Moment 26	Simon Lewis
Moment 27	Michael Turner
Moment 28	Simon Lewis
Moment 29	Ferret Fotographics
Moment 30	Ferret Fotographics
Moment 31	Ferret Fotographics
Moment 32	Michael Turner
Moment 33	Michael Turner
Moment 34	BRDC Archives/www.brdc.co.uk
Moment 35	BRDC Archives/www.brdc.co.uk
Moment 36	Jim Bamber
Moment 39	www.peteaustinphoto.co.uk
Moment 40	Ferret Fotographics
Moment 41	Ferret Fotographics
Moment 42	Simon Lewis
Moment 43	Ed McDonough
Moment 44	www.peteaustinphoto.co.uk
Moment 45	www.peteaustinphoto.co.uk
Moment 46	BRDC Archives/www.brdc.co.uk
Moment 47	BRDC Archives/www.brdc.co.uk
Moment 48	Mike Jiggle Archive
Moment 49	Courtesy of Bentley Motors
Moment 50	Ferret Fotographics
Moment 51	Mike Jiggle Archive
Moment 52	Mike Jiggle Archive
Moment 54	Jim Bamber
Moment 55	www.peteaustinphoto.co.uk
Moment 56	Mike Jiggle Archive
Moment 57	Courtesy Mike Coombe
Moment 58	Ferret Fotographics
Moment 59	Mike Jiggle Archive
Moment 60	LAT Photographic
Moment 61	Michael Turner
Moment 62	Ferret Fotographics
Moment 63	BRDC Archives/www.brdc.co.uk
Moment 64	Courtesy of Texaco
Moment 65	BRDC Archives/www.brdc.co.uk
Moment 66	BRDC Archives/www.brdc.co.uk and Mike Jiggle
Moment 68	Ed McDonough
Moment 69	BRDC Archives/www.brdc.co.uk
Moment 72	Mike Jiggle Archive
Moment 73	Michael Turner
Moment 74	LAT Photographic
Moment 75	Ferret Fotographics
Moment 76	Mike Jiggle Archive
Moment 78	Jim Bamber
Moment 81	Ferret Fotographics
Moment 82	Ferret Fotographics
Moment 83	Mike Jiggle Archive
Moment 84	Courtesy of Jack Fairman
Moment 85	Mike Jiggle Archive
Moment 86	Courtesy of Honda
Moment 87	Mike Jiggle Archive
Moment 88	Simon Lewis
Moment 89	Mike Jiggle Archive
Moment 92	Mike Jiggle Archive
Moment 93	Ferret Fotographics
Moment 94	Mike Jiggle Archive
Moment 95	BRDC Archives/www.brdc.co.uk
Moment 96	Ferret Fotographics
Moment 97	Ferret Fotographics
Moment 99	BRDC Archives/www.brdc.co.uk
Moment 101	BRDC Archives/www.brdc.co.uk
Moment 102	Simon Lewis
Moment 103	Mike Jiggle Archive
Moment 104	Michael Turner
Moment 106	BRDC Archives/www.brdc.co.uk
Moment 107	Jim Bamber
Moment 108	BRDC Archives/www.brdc.co.uk
Moment 110	Michael Turner
Moment 111	Michael Turner
Moment 112	Ferret Fotographics
Moment 113	Ferret Fotographics
Moment 114	Ferret Fotographics
Moment 115	Mike Jiggle Archive
Moment 116	Mike Jiggle Archive
Moment 118	Mike Jiggle Archive
Moment 119	BRDC Archives/www.brdc.co.uk
Moment 120	Simon Lewis
Moment 121	Jim Bamber
Moment 122	www.peteaustinphoto.co.uk
Moment 123	Michael Turner
Moment 124	Ferret Fotographics
Moment 125	www.peteaustinphoto.co.uk
Moment 126	Michael Turner
Moment 127	Michael Turner
Moment 129	Courtesy of Renault
Moment 130	Jim Bamber
Moment 131	Ferret Fotographics
Moment 132	Courtesy of Renault
Moment 133	Mike Jiggle Archive
Moment 135	Mike Jiggle Archive
Moment 136	Simon Lewis
Moment 138	Jim Bamber
Moment 140	www.peteaustinphoto.co.uk
Moment 141	www.peteaustinphoto.co.uk
Moment 142	Mike Jiggle Archive
Moment 143	BRDC Archives/www.brdc.co.uk
Moment 144	Michael Turner
Moment 145	www.peteaustinphoto.co.uk
Moment 147	Ferret Fotographics
Moment 148	Mike Jiggle Archive
Moment 151	Ferret Fotographics
Moment 152	Ferret Fotographics
Moment 153	BRDC Archives/www.brdc.co.uk
Moment 154	Ed McDonough
Moment 155	Ferret Fotographics
Moment 156	Courtesy of Bentley Motors
Moment 157	www.peteaustinphoto.co.uk
Moment 158	Ferret Fotographics
Moment 160	Courtesy of RAC
Moment 161	BRDC Archives/www.brdc.co.uk
Moment 162	www.peteaustinphoto.co.uk
Moment 163	Courtesy of Innes Marlow
Moment 164	Mike Jiggle Archive
Moment 165	Ferret Fotographics
Moment 166	BRDC Archives/www.brdc.co.uk